THE ECOLOGICAL ECLAIR

Recipes for Sugarless Treats

Frances Sheridan Goulart

MACMILLAN PUBLISHING CO., INC.
NEW YORK

COLLIER MACMILLAN PUBLISHERS
LONDON

This book is dedicated
to my second born,
Steffan Eamon

Macmillan Publishing Co., Inc.
866 Third Avenue, New York, N.Y. 10022
Collier-Macmillan Canada Ltd.

Library of Congress Cataloging in Publication Data
Goulart, Frances Sheridan.
The ecological eclair.

Includes index.
1. Sugar-free diet. I. Title.
RM237.9.G68   641.5′638   74-23196
ISBN 0-02-544910-9

First Printing 1975

Printed in the United States of America

Contents

Appendix

Introduction

If all the 100,000 dentists in the United States restored decayed teeth day and night, 365 days a year, as many new cavities would have formed at the end of the year as were just restored during the previous year.
—Dr. Abraham E. Nizel, Tufts University
School of Dental Medicine

The sweet tooth has fallen on hard times. According to a recent study by the Senate Select Committee on Nutrition and Human Needs, "Tooth Decay is now the country's most widespread health problem. . . . The average American's consumption of sugar and corn syrup is 115 pounds annually. . . . Food processors in this country increased the use of sugar in their products by 50% during the decade from 1950 to 1960."

Among its evils, refined sugar in all its forms disrupts the hormonal level of the blood and distorts the calcium-phosphorus relationship in the body (it has been recently demonstrated, for instance, that nine chocolates will throw the body's calcium-phosphorus level out of balance within two and a half hours of ingestion and keep it below the margin of safety for immunity to dental decay for at least seventy-two hours); it has exhibited addictive properties, and it is definitely linked to the production of kidney stones, allergies, diabetes and heart disease. And there is evidence, according to White House nutritionist Dr. Jean Mayer, that sugar-rich snack foods may be causing nutritional deficiencies of such necessary trace elements as chromium and zinc. Indeed, Dr. John Yudkin, the eminent British biochemist and author of an exhaustive study of sugar's ills, titled *Sweet and Dangerous,* says that a high sugar intake may be the single most important factor in the production of artery-clogging blood fats. "If only a fraction of what is already known about the effects of sugar were to be revealed in relation to any other material used as a food additive," says Yudkin, "that material would be promptly banned."

Sugar, according to Dr. John Prutting, a New York internist, lowers vital mineral levels such as potassium and magnesium in the blood serum. These play an important role in the functioning of the heart, the brain, and other organs. Sugar needs these minerals to be metabolized and if they are not present in foods, they will be taken from other parts of the body. This can lead to malfunctions of organs such as heart irregularities and muscle cramps. And in the opinion of Dr. Denis Burkitt, of the Medical Research Council of Great Britain, eating white bread and soft drinks containing sugar increases an individual's susceptibility to colon cancer (the second most common malignancy in America today).

What is offered the public euphemistically as "sugar replacement" may be even worse. The safeness of saccharin, a chemical sweetener 500 times sweeter than sugar, is in serious question at this time. There is concern about its possible ill effects on the nervous system, the heart, and unborn children. Saccharin is made from a sulfonizol, and, like drugs containing the compound, can cause allergic and toxic reactions affecting the skin, heart rhythms and gastrointestinal tract. Adverse effects on the kidneys have been observed after a single excessive dose, notes Dr. Hyman Gordon of the Southern California Permanente Medical Group. It is also important to remember that different formulations of saccharin contain different impurities. One of the common contaminants, a manufacturing by-product called sulfonamide, is closely related to a known cancer-causing substance. In the opinion of the American Association for the Advancement of Science, saccharin (which they found caused more dangerous tumors in laboratory mice than cyclamate) should be banned posthaste. The fact that saccharin has been in widespread use for close to a hundred years bestows no margin of safety. Cyclamate, the now-banned noncaloric chemical, had been in widespread use for thirty years prior to disclosure of its many deleterious effects.

Because sugar is a powerful stimulant, it has the same relationship to food that alcohol has to milk. It oxidizes rapidly and violently in the stomach upon the slightest encounter with oxygen and produces an explosive effect upon the digestive system.

Sugar is a starvation food, a chemical—a drug, if you will—and it is artificial in the extreme, containing no vitamins or minerals at all. "Commercial sugar," says Los Angeles physician Phillip M. Lovell, "is representative of the ultimate extreme in food degradation. Merely to state that it is a starvation food is putting it mildly. Sugar is the most injurious product in our national dietary with no exceptions and under every possible condition."

As for corn syrup and the frequently lauded, supposedly beneficial glucose, several American nutritionists now report that glucose is the only sugar known absolutely to cause diabetes in test animals. Corn syrup is another unnatural sweetener made by treating cornstarch with sulphuric acid, neutralizing it with sodium carbonate, and finally filtering it through beef bones to clarify it. Corn syrup has two aliases: commercial glucose or dextrose. It is cheaper than sugar and is even more rapidly assimilated by the body than other sugars.

Refined sugar (including brown sugar, which most often is no more than white sugar gussied up with a bit of molasses or caramel coloring) is a major component in most of our fractionated foods today. According to *Agricultural Research,* published by the USDA, "Beverages alone, primarily soft drinks, comprise the largest single use of refined sugar, accounting for over one-fifth of the total refined sugar in the U.S. diet." A recent *Boys' Life* magazine survey of its readers revealed that the average Boy Scout drinks more than three bottles of soda pop a day and that one in twelve Scouts drinks an amazing total of eight or more bottles daily.

To make matters worse, sugar is "hidden" (thanks to the government's Standards of Identity code) in everything from yogurt to mayonnaise, corned beef hash, peanut butter, pet foods, lunch meats, salad dressings and soy sauce, as well as some highly regarded "health foods" such as commercial Tiger's milk. (Why not make your own? See recipe herein, page 74.) In the very foods, in other words, on which our infants and children are supposedly nurtured. Some serious questions arise: If, as the *Journal of American Dietetics* tells us, "Refined white sugar interferes with the absorption of calcium and protein," what's it doing in our children's cookies and hot chocolate? And if, as the *Journal of Nutrition* tells us, "All infant formulas should contain some milk sugar (lactose). Other sugars (refined sugar) should be avoided," what's it doing in every commercially available baby formula? Recent studies indicate that many a baby begun on sugar-sweetened formulas (as most babies are) develops abnormal fat cells which lead to weight problems that will dog him all his days.

So, what is the alternative? Certainly not "raw" sugar. According to Fred Rohe, a leading natural foods merchant, "raw sugar," as sold to the public, is actually refined sugar with molasses added. Genuine unrefined sugar is an impure product that still has 30 to 40 percent of the original nutritional value of the sugarcane. It has been illegal in this country since 1948 because of the unsanitary conditions under which it is processed.

Certainly no alternative is offered by saccharin or any of its analogs. (We might note with shame that our children counted among the heavy consumers of all that nonnutritive cyclamate sweetening we Americans consumed during the boom years of 1955–1969—17 million pounds of it in 1969 alone.)

The alternatives are the *natural sweeteners* whose names follow, along with their respectable credentials. This book endorses *no* unnatural foods, eschewing chocolate, white flour and all other refined food ingredients. As opposed to the largely chemical concoctions which today's storebought sweets have become (and especially candy bars, on which we are spending twice as much as on fresh vegetables these nonsalad days), sweetstuffs made from natural sweeteners and other natural foodstuffs will be nontoxic and nutritious. And best of all, since they originate in your own kitchen rather than in the laboratories of a conscienceless conglomerate, you can fortify and enrich them in any manner you like with any desired balance of vitamins and minerals.

How easy is it to give up sugar completely?

According to Professor Aharon Mordecai Cohen, who has spent thirteen years in sugar studies at the Hadassah Medical Research Center in Jerusalem, "sugar is like salt and smoking, simply a matter of habit."

To those of us who believe that "sugaring off," in the sense of abandoning the use of refined sugar utterly (*not* in the sense that the maple sugar industry uses this term to describe the act of turning maple sap into sugar), is a habit worth acquiring, this book is dedicated, as a sort of first-aid manual.

The proof will be in the pudding. Or in this case, in the eclair.

Eat on.

Frances Sheridan Goulart
Wilton, Connecticut
1974

A Note to the Reader

Now that we have decided to put sugar firmly behind us, what do we put before us—in our coffee cups, our cereal bowls, our Easter baskets?

Please read about all the alternatives presently available in the section entitled STOCKING UP. You may even wish to try making a few sugars of your own. HOMEMADE SUGARS tells you how. More importantly perhaps, you will find an Inventory of Ingredients in STOCKING UP which provides a brief profile of the many less-than-everyday ingredients used throughout the book: triticale flour, dried rosebuds, butter extract, peanut meal—what they are and where they can be gotten by mail, if your local natural food shop doesn't carry them. Also, this section explains once and for all what exactly is meant when "oil" or "vanilla extract" or "baby flour" and other frequent terms are used. Then go on to the recipes, bearing in mind that should you wind up with an extra cup of Tiger's milk or some yet-nourishing remnants of apple pie, a section called RECYCLING NOTES (referred to at the foot of some recipes) will tell you how to put them to good, ecological, economical use once more.

SOURCES is a brief shopping list of places to write away to for harder-to-find ingredients.

And then there is SUGARING OFF, a section in five parts which you will encounter off and on throughout the book because that's the way it occurs. It is simply an "intermission" between recipes, a miscellany of hints, statistics and such as they pertain to the sweet life.

The recipes hopefully speak for themselves.

STOCKING UP

STOCKING UP

MAJOR NATURAL SWEETENERS
(Storebought)

Honey

Chemistry: With only one exception (date syrup, which has a slightly higher caloric count), honey surpasses all other natural foods as a source of heat and energy. The only truly natural (unmanufactured) sweetener, it consists of two monosaccharides, or simple sugars: dextrose, which is used to replace the oxygen burned up by lactic acid in the course of the body's activities; and levulose (or fructose), the sweetest and mildest of sugars, of which there are few natural sources in the modern diet. Honey is an important antifatigue food since it is predigested, builds up the alkaline reserves in the blood and tissues, and provides a maximum of energy with a minimum of shock to the digestive system. Sugar-laden foods overload the bloodstream in fifteen minutes; honey is absorbed over a period of four hours. Besides protein from the pollen (the substance responsible for clouding in unfiltered honey), good honey contains some vitamin A, several vitamins from the B complex, and vital enzymes and minerals such as phosphorus, potassium, calcium, sodium, sulphur, iron, magnesium and manganese —all in the right small amounts and balance to serve the needs of the normal individual. In addition, honey has antiseptic and hygroscopic properties, which means it draws moisture from anything it comes in contact with, including harmful micro-organisms—no disease germs can survive in honey over a few hours.

History: One of the oldest foods known to man (cave paintings from prehistoric times show man in pursuit of the honeycomb), honey preceded cereals and milk as a daily food. Four thousand years ago, all candy was made with honey. Honey was both a symbol of purity and goodness (it was seriously doubted that happiness awaited any man who was not greeted at birth with a vessel of honey) and a universally accepted medium of exchange (honey was used almost exclusively in ancient Mediterranean communities in place of gold and silver). Of the nutritional and medicinal values of honey no ancient scribe has written more than Pliny the Elder, who said, "Powdered bees with milk, wine or honey will surely cure dropsy, dissolve gravel stones and cure the stopping of the bladder."

Types and Varieties: Honey is made from the nectar of more than 1,800 species of plants, trees and shrubs. There are 6,000 kinds of honey, 250 of which are produced in the United States, and of that number perhaps less than twenty-five varieties are readily available to the general public. Honey varies widely from one region to another in regard to taste, aroma, and consistency. Perhaps as much as 70 percent of the honey sold in the United States is clover (there are several types), mildest of the varieties. Three thousand seven hundred nectar loads go into the production of a single pound of honey, while a bee must consume six or seven pounds of honey to produce one pound of beeswax. (The chewing of the comb, incidentally, is beneficial to sinus and hay fever congestion.) The darker honeys have a higher mineral content than amber-colored types like tupelo. Buckwheat honey, for example, has four times the iron of lighter honeys.

Heather honey from Scotland is thick, aromatic and valued for its unusual mineral properties. The clover honeys of Ohio, Michigan and New York are considered blessed with a near-ideal consistency. Grapefruit blossom honey of Texas is rated as possibly the finest of domestic honeys; it is pungent, beautiful and spicy. The sourwood honey of Tennessee and North Carolina also has its partisans, as does the peppermint-flavored basswood honey. Although one-crop honey is the rule, mixed honeys (produced by the bees from several types of blossoms) are sometimes available. These should not be confused with blended honeys, which are produced by combining two or more honeys with different but complementary flavors, such as orange blossom, sage and clover. Because of their high levulose content, honeys such as firewood, tupelo and sage will not granulate, whereas the opposite is true of such honeys as buckwheat, clover, alfalfa and others which are high in dextrose.

Baking and Storing: According to knowledgeable herbalists, refined commercial honey is sugary in the mouth, whereas a good natural honey will prick the throat when swallowed. It is a good rule to buy only unpasteurized, unfiltered honey.

Heating (a process intended only for the cosmetic purpose of inhibiting crystallization) destroys enzymes and robs honey of its nutrients. Except for buckwheat, honey loses its characteristic flavor with heating. Alas! However, honey may be frozen for long periods without damage. Granulation is not a sign of spoilage, but an indication that you have purchased a high-quality unpasteurized honey.

If you want to be sure that a honey is fully ripened and will not ferment, up-end the jar; a large air bubble should rise from the cap to the bottom. The slower it moves, the richer the honey. Stickiness (viscosity) is a sign that a good fluid honey has fully matured. Cloudiness is due to the presence of pollen which imparts important protein, enzymes and nutrients of its own.

Why are some honeys pleasantly liquid and others annoyingly thick? Place of origin is one explanation. Honey made by bees in arid country is much thicker than honey made where rainfall is ample. And nectar may be more concentrated in dry weather when most of the pollen is picked up by the bees.

Well-capped honey will not ferment if it is kept in a dry place. Good honey has a naturally long shelf-life. It will improve in flavor and aroma as the months, even years, pass. The best insurance that your honey is free from traces of pesticides? Purchase only desert, mountain or wildflower varieties.

1 TABLESPOON: 60 CALORIES / 7 CARBOHYDRATES

Unsulphured Molasses

This is not a by-product of the sugar-making process but a deliberately manufactured food, made from the juice of sun-ripened cane which has grown from twelve to fifteen months. It is also known as first extraction molasses. The quality of unsulphured molasses depends largely on the type of sugar used and its place in the first steps of the refining process. Choicest varieties come from Barbados, Antigua, Puerto Rico and Louisiana. It is well supplied with B vitamins (except for folic acid and B_1 which are destroyed in the heating process), calcium, phosphorus and iron, but it is only one-tenth as nutritive as blackstrap molasses. Unsulphured molasses imparts a taffylike flavor to baked goods, but if more than a quarter-cup of sweetness is called for in a recipe, molasses may be a poor choice. Baked goods made with molasses stay moist and keep longer than sugar-sweetened foods.

1 TABLESPOON: 50 CALORIES / 13 CARBOHYDRATES

Note: Bypass sulphured molasses, which is a by-product of sugar-making, a process in which noxious sulphur fumes are used—hence the name.

Blackstrap Molasses

Also called third extraction molasses, this is a rich source of thiamine (B_1), a vitamin which must be replenished daily. This sweetener contains thirty times more nutrients than cane sugar. It has 258 mg. calcium in five tablespoons (milk has only 120), more iron than eggs, more potassium than any other food. Minerals and heat-stable vitamins are ten times more concentrated than in first or second extraction molasses. It is an effective remedy for anemia and constipation (because of its high levels of inositol, a B vitamin) and some forms of arthritis (because of the "Wurzen Factor" which is also part of its nutritional makeup). It is also the best-known repository of B_6 (the vitamin which activates seventy-five different enzyme systems in the body).

1 TABLESPOON: 45 CALORIES / 11 CARBOHYDRATES

Maple Syrup

"Pure" maple syrup is an outstanding source of potassium and calcium and is also rich in sodium and phosphorus. About forty gallons of maple sap are required to make one gallon of syrup, which explains its seemingly high price. Although Vermont and maple syrup are synonymous in the public mind, New York State, Ohio and Quebec (Canada) also rank high as major maple syrup-producing regions. Nutritionally speaking, syrup from Canadian sources is your best bet since bacterial and antifoaming agents are often used during processing in this country (in addition to formaldehyde pellets to keep tapholes open). Most Canadian brands are processed without pellets.

Once opened, maple syrup must be properly covered and stored in the refrigerator, where it will last a month or two. Maple sugar, however, is pantry shelf stuff and as such has a long life. It should keep nicely for as long as a year.

1 TABLESPOON: 50 CALORIES / 12 CARBOHYDRATES

Note: What is true of the syrup is also largely true of maple sugar—which you would probably restrict anyway because of high price and low availability—and maple cream, which is even scarcer and less likely to be found in its natural, unsugared state.

Sorghum

Fifty years ago the production of sorghum in this country was 20 million gallons. Today it is hardly a tenth of that. At one time in our pioneer past, almost every family kept a sorghum jar and its use was widespread in the 1800s. Sorghum's decline in popularity paralleled the rise in the use of cane and beet sugars. Sorghum syrup is made from sorghum grass, the seeds of which are used as feed grain and resemble Indian corn. It is a soy-sauce-colored syrup which rivals molasses for stickiness and which is sold in traditional syrup-shaped bottles (or occasionally quart jars, and even by the pound from some mail order sources) at about twice the price of supermarket molasses. An abundant source of minerals, sorghum is rich in calcium, phosphorus, riboflavin and niacin. It ranks next to liver as a source of iron.

1 TABLESPOON: 36 CALORIES / 6 CARBOHYDRATES

Carob Syrup and Carob Powder

The carob bean is a fruit dating back to biblical times. It is roasted and ground to powder, making it an unusual auxiliary sweetener rather than a replacement for sugar or honey (its flavor is often described as maltlike or fruitlike). Also known as honey locust or St. John's bread, the carob pod produces a light or a dark syrup slightly less sweet than honey. Carob is an ideal replacement for chocolate (which is objectionable because it contains sugar, caffein, artificial flavoring and vanillin, an artificial flavoring extract). As such, it has one-half the calories, one one-hundredth of the fat, and two and a half times more calcium than chocolate (among its negative qualities, chocolate inhibits the absorption of calcium by the body). Carob is high in niacin, thiamine, riboflavin and pectin (the nutrient that exerts a powerful force against radio-active poisoning and also stabilizes blood cholesterol levels). High in natural sugar and low in starch, carob is noted for its usefulness in alleviating diarrhea. It contains the same nutritive properties as barley and is often fed to cattle when that vitamin-rich grain is in short supply.

Light or dark carob syrup is available at perhaps twice the price of a good honey. The dark syrup more closely resembles the flavor of chocolate sauce.

1 TABLESPOON: 30 CALORIES / 6 CARBOHYDRATES

Date Syrup and Date Sugar

Like honey, the date—man's oldest cultivated fruit—is an outstanding energy food, high in potassium and low in sodium. The vitamin B complex and vitamin A are also well represented. Because it is 75 percent carbohydrate, high in roughage and very alkaline, it should be used in moderation. The syrup is formulated from fresh dates, the sugar from dried dates. It is slightly more expensive and slightly less versatile (because of its coarser texture) than honey. Note that date sugar does not dissolve in liquid like granulated sugar, and therefore is not always a suitable substitute.

1 TABLESPOON: 36 CALORIES / 24 CARBOHYDRATES

Note: Date chips or flakes, made from very dry dates and available at health food stores, make a fine natural candy snack.

Other Dried Fruits

Papaya pulp is a good buy, should you come across a jar. Papayas are scarce in their fresh or dried forms but are highly regarded for their enzymatic properties. And what's to stop you from making your own apricot, fig, prune or apple sugar? All you need are very, very dry fruit and a very sturdy blender (you must use the chop-and-stop method) or better yet, a coffee grinder or electric food mill.

MINOR NATURAL SWEETENERS
(Storebought)

Barley Malt, Dry Malt, Malt Extract

These concentrated infusions of germinated barley are made into syrups, powders or liquids. The barley is sprouted, dried and ground. Germination changes the grain so that it dissolves easily. Light malt is used in its natural state; the darker variety has been dried or roasted. Because of its enzyme content, malt is often used as a food for infants. It has many of the same nutritional benefits as barley and milk solids. Although excellent for fortifying and supplementing daily diets, its use should be limited because of its highly concentrated state. A commercially available barley malt sweetener sold in spice jars is supplemented with saccharin and is therefore unacceptable.

1 TABLESPOON: 31 CALORIES / 7 CARBOHYDRATES

Pure Granulated Honey Powder

At about 40¢ per ounce, this isn't practical for use as a wide-spectrum sweetener but it's nice to know about for special uses. One firm packages it with supplementary powdered vitamin C.

NUTRITIONAL VALUES: UNKNOWN

Fruit Sugar (Fructose)

This 99 percent pure natural fruit sugar is recommended with reservations since the remaining percent is a chemical called sorbitol, found in many fruits and berries. Large amounts of sorbitol, which is 60 percent as sweet as sugar, have a mild laxative effect, but tests have indicated the additive to be otherwise unharmful. Fructose dissolves more easily than date sugar and is nearly twice as sweet as cane sugar. But it is costly at approximately 22¢ an ounce.

1 TABLESPOON: 22 CALORIES / CARBOHYDRATES:
UNKNOWN

Coconut Shreds, Meal, Beverage Powder

The meat and milk of this nut are enzyme-rich and the oil is a good substitute for butter if you aren't concerned about the 34 grams of saturated fat in each cup. The milk contains vitamins A, C and G, as well as vitamin D, which is rarely found in foods. It is also a good source of iodine, phosphorus and calcium. But be aware that sugar lurks in any brand that is not broadcast as "unsweetened."

1 TABLESPOON: 10 CALORIES / 2 CARBOHYDRATES

Organic Carrot Syrup

This is another expensive curiosity. The price is admittedly dear ($2.00 for eight ounces) but if you truly like the sweet-potato taste of canned carrot juice, imagine it in a sweeter, more viscous state, and then decide whether or not to treat yourself to a jar. It takes eleven pounds of carrots to make one pound of desiccated carrots and thus to make carrot syrup, so perhaps $2.00 is practically token payment. It is made from carrot sugars and crude malt, and you can make your own. (See recipe for Vegetarian's Butter #2, page 138.)

Fruit Concentrates

Beyond the orange juice concentrate in your freezer, there are cherry, fig, raspberry, even pomegranate concentrates (usually sold in eight- or sixteen-ounce jars) which, when used undiluted, bestow a fresh if low-octane sweetness to so many things. In conjunction with spices or flavor extracts, they sometimes eliminate the need for further sweetening.

NUTRITIONAL VALUES: SEE SPECIFIC JUICE

Flavoring Extracts

One teaspoon of pure vanilla replaces the same amount of vanillin (a synthetic flavoring agent that may contain creosote and lignin, a wood byproduct). But even pure vanilla might not be pure, since most imported vanilla beans are treated with glycerin. Read labels and consider the possibility of brewing your own extracts. A recipe for homemade vanilla appears on page 24, under *Other Home-made Sweeteners*. Also see Sweet Nothing on page 19 for an alternative to artificial orange extract.

There are at least half a hundred extracts available (a fair percentage of them the real thing). You can also blend extracts by fusing what seem to be two compatible flavors—almond and vanilla are the two most often combined. It is an informal but not immutable rule that spices and extracts do not abide in the same recipe. And, as a rule, the only extract used with carob is vanilla.

HOMEMADE SUGARS

There are few substitutes for granulated sugar. Two are commercially available, but how much date sugar and fructose can you afford to use? So, how about some homemade granulated sugars to provide some nonempty calories and some semi-sweetness. Bear in mind that none of the natural sugars are absolute analogs for any of the unnatural refined ones (i.e., brown sugar, corn syrup, confectioners sugar and so on). They will not have the same dissolving properties, nor in most cases will they be nearly as sweet. Each of the following "recipes" makes one cup. Store sugar in a screw-top jar and refrigerate.

White Sugar

Sift together ¼ cup each whey powder, lactose powder and arrowroot starch, and combine with ¼ cup fine unsweetened coconut meal. You may substitute ½ cup noninstant dry milk powder for the whey and lactose if you wish.

Enriched White Sugar

In the above recipe, replace coconut meal with ¼ cup finely ground white sesame seeds (sesame meal contains four times more magnesium and ten times more calcium than sunflower seeds and is an important source of a more easily assimilated form of lecithin than that available from soybeans).

Dark Brown Sugar

Granulate 1 cup of date sugar in the blender until it is fine and powdery. Or you may replace ¼ cup of it with ¼ cup toasted ground flaxseed.

Light Brown Sugar

Granulate ½ cup date sugar and combine with ¼ cup finely ground natural brown sesame seeds and ¼ cup noninstant dry milk powder.

Red Sugar

Combine ¼ cup Fruit Salt (recipe in this section) with ¼ cup sifted rose hip powder and ½ cup lactose, whey or milk powder.

Children's Sugar (or Chocolate Sugar)

Combine ¼ cup sifted carob powder with ¼ cup sifted unsweetened malted milk powder and ½ cup noninstant milk powder (¼ cup of this may be replaced with granulated coconut meal).

Sea Sugar

Combine ¼ cup of finely powdered (granulate in your blender) kelp or dulse (or other dried seaweed) with ¼ cup toasted wheat germ and ¼ cup blender-ground granola. (Seaweed adds a multitude of minerals and the granola will make up for the missing sweetness.)

Praline Sugar

Combine ½ cup finely ground raw or toasted almonds with ½ cup finely granulated date sugar.

Dry Roasted Sugar

In skillet in a 300° oven, toast ¼ cup raw peanuts, ¼ cup sunflower seeds and ¼ cup raw cashews for 20 minutes. Grind in blender and combine with ¼ cup unsweetened coconut meal.

Liquid Sugar

Buzz in blender: ¼ cup liquid honey with ¾ cup fruit juice concentrate.

How to Use Homemade Sugar: On toast (any of the above are splendid variations on the cinnamon toast theme), on top of sliced fruit, over ice cream, and as part of or all of the sweetening in some of the recipes that follow in this book.

OTHER HOMEMADE SWEETENERS

Sweet Nothing (a homemade flavoring extract)

Dilute 4 ounces of orange juice concentrate, cherry concentrate or any sugar-free fruit concentrate with 1½ cups water. Boil in an uncovered saucepan until liquid is reduced to about 4 tbsp.

This extract is a delicious plus in pies (as part of the sweetening syrup usually called for) or as a glaze on coffee cakes, sweet rolls, quick breads, and as otherwise indicated in the recipes in this book.

Sweet Something (a homemade unbuttered butter)

1 large egg yolk *
1 cup cold-pressed oil
any type of honey, to
    taste

approx. ¼ tsp. almond
    extract

* See Recycling Note #5

Warm the yolk to room temperature and beat it well. Add oil (at room temperature, too) drop by drop (as though you were making mayonnaise). When mixture thickens, add honey to taste (the mixture will become beautifully translucent at this point) and almond extract, if desired. Makes an éclair filling with éclat, if you are toastless.

Fortified Water or Sweet Stock

Use any of the following:

pot liquor from soaking dried fruits
leftover herb tea (sweetened or not)
diluted fruit juice
water or milk used for cooking pasta or grains
water used for soaking nuts or bran
whey left from homemade cheese making
sprout soaking water
water used to stew or poach fruits
pureed soft, ripe summer squash

Calcium Cooking Water

#1 Save your eggshells and put them into a kettle with water to cover and a teaspoon of lemon juice (to extract the calcium). Mash with potato masher and bring to boil. Simmer 20 minutes and strain. Refrigerate and use as needed.

#2 Pack wide-mouth Mason jars full of cut-up bones and fill with water. Close jars and process in pressure cooker at 10–12 pounds pressure. (The greater the pressure, the more gelatin will cook out into liquid.) Allow to cool. Open jars, skim off fat and remove any bone pieces. Dilute with a bit of water and whip in blender.

Whipped Water

Put warm plain or fortified water into blender with gelatin powder (2 tbsp. to 1 cup water). Process at medium speed, turn to high, and beat until white and foamy.

Mixed Honey

Combine honey with another sweetener, such as 1 part date sugar to 1 part honey; 1 part sorghum to 3 parts honey; or 1 part blackstrap molasses to 3 parts honey.

Blended Honey

Blend together two or more varieties of honey, such as: sage and clover or alfalfa and buckwheat.

Half-and-Half Honey or Skimmed Honey

Blend 1/3 cup water with 1 cup honey for maple-syrup consistency.

Blend 1/5 cup water with 1 cup honey for cane-syrup consistency.

Mixed Molasses

Blend blackstrap molasses with unsulphured molasses, half and half or in any proportions that please your palate.

Carob Syrup

Mix ¼ cup carob powder with ⅓ cup date sugar. Add 2 tbsp. dry malt (optional), ⅔ cup milk, and a pinch of salt. Bring to a boil and simmer 5 minutes. Add ½ tsp. pure vanilla extract.

Store in refrigerator.

Fruit Syrup #1

In a double boiler, melt ½ cup soy or dairy butter. Whip in 1 cup honey. Add 1 quart fresh fruit juice and heat until a syrupy consistency is reached.

Fruit Syrup #2

Puree 2 pounds of any fresh fruit (removing skins, pits, cores where pertinent) and add to ½ cup melted soy or dairy butter. Add 1 cup warmed honey and dilute as necessary with a little water. A little lemon juice will sharpen flavors, too.

Fruit Syrup #3

Pour 1½ cups fortified water (recipe on page 20) over 1 cup dried apricots, prunes, apples or other dried fruit. Allow to stew overnight. Put fruit and water in blender with ½ cup warm honey and ⅔ cup melted dairy or soy butter, and blend.

Note: All of the above fruit syrups should be stored in screw-top jars in the refrigerator. Should you fancy the sturdier flavor, you may substitute ¼ cup sorghum or molasses for ¼ cup of the honey specified.

Semi-Sorghum

For newcomers to this highly nutritious homespun natural sweetener, a period of initiation might be necessary. Try this: Blend ½ cup wildflower or clover honey with ½ cup sorghum and ¼ cup fortified water (recipe on page 20). Welcomed even by those who haven't been fully weaned from Girl Scout cookies.

Fruit Butter #1

Put 2 cups pineapple chunks and 2 chopped, cored apples into blender with just enough juice to process into a thick butter. Decant, add honey to taste and store in covered refrigerator dish.

Fruit Butter #2

Put ½ cup raw almonds and ½ cup fortified water (see page 20) into blender and reduce to a liquid paste. Add 1 cup peeled and pitted peaches or apricots, ½ cup household honey, and a pinch of anise or allspice. Blend until smooth and store covered in refrigerator.

Fruit Salt

Grind together, till powdery fine (a seed mill is best tool for maceration), sun- or oven-dried peels from organically-grown tangerines, oranges, lemons, grapefruit or kumquats. Store in airtight jar in refrigerator. This will keep 1–2 weeks. Use as directed (in the following recipes), if warranted or wanted.

Flower Syrup

Combine in a saucepan 1 cup water, ½ cup orange juice, 1 cup honey, 1 tbsp. mixed flower tea leaves, and ½ tsp. lemon juice. Bring to a boil and continue boiling until liquid is reduced by half. Refrigerate. Adds aromatic sweetness to baked and other goods.

Homemade Vanilla

Cut 2 vanilla beans into small pieces. Whiz in blender with ⅔ cup warm liquid whey or water and 1 tbsp. honey. Bring to a boil in covered pan and immediately put into a clean jar with tight lid. Let stand overnight, then strain it into the blender. Mix 2 tsp. lecithin with 2 tsp. oil and 1 tsp. honey. Slowly add this to blender while processing at low speed. Pour into two 2-ounce bottles and keep refrigerated.

Maple Cream

Heat maple syrup to 232 degrees. Remove from heat and cool quickly to room temperature. Stir until it forms fine granules and becomes thick and creamy (about 20 minutes). Fine simply as a bread spread (but other uses suggested in the following recipes).

Sugarless Protein Powder

½ cup noninstant milk powder
1 tbsp. lecithin granules or flakes
¼ cup food yeast
2 tbsp. fruit salt (see recipe, page 23)

2 tbsp. homemade sugar (see recipe, page 16)
2 tbsp. banana flakes (optional)
2 tbsp. wheat germ or bran flakes

Blend everything and refrigerate.

Some More Natural Sweeteners

Parsnips become incredibly sweet when cooked (steaming is best); the longer the better (45 mins.) . . . a bananalike flavor, say connoisseurs.

Cooked Squash can taste even sweeter than fruit . . . to perform this small vegetarian miracle, cook and puree some yams or winter squash and use a cup or more in place of the fruit in an applesauce cake.

Amasake Syrup is made from fermented rice and worth a try if you have oriental connections.

Vanilla Beans have a far more potent flavor than flavorings or extracts. Split lengthwise, they can be added to any liquid you are simmering as part of any dessert. They may be used several times until their strength is diminished.

THIS FOR THAT
(Substitutions and Equivalents)

Sugars

1¼ cups maple syrup *
1⅓ cups maple sugar
¾ cup honey **
1 cup molasses *   =   1 cup white sugar
1½ cups date syrup *
1½ cups sorghum *
1¼ cups carob syrup *
2 cups date sugar
½ cup plus ½ cup each honey and date sugar***

See other natural sweetener combinations under *Homemade Sugars*, page 16.

* *reduce liquid by ½ cup*
** *reduce liquid by ¼ cup*
*** *reduce liquid by ⅛ cup*

Syrups

For maple-syrup consistency, dilute 1 cup honey with ⅓ cup water. Warm both before blending.

For corn-syrup consistency, dilute 1 cup honey with 1/5 cup water (for coffee, cereal, pancakes, fruit drinks).

Baking with Honey

If substituting honey for sugar: Always lower oven temperature 25 degrees; add 4 tbsp. additional flour in recipes where crispness is important, or whenever no liquids are called for.

Weight Equivalents

1 cup honey = ¾ lb.
1 cup molasses = approx. ¾ lb.
2½ cups raisins = 1 lb.
2 cups dates = 1 lb.
3 tbsp. carob powder plus 1 tbsp. milk and 1 tbsp. water = 1 oz. bitter chocolate

Flavoring and Extract Equivalents

Banana	½ tsp. = approx. ½ cup bananas
Cherry	½ tsp. = approx. ½ cup cherries
Cinnamon	½ tsp. = approx. 1 tsp. ground cinnamon
Ginger	½ tsp. = approx. 1 tsp. ground ginger
Lemon	1½ tsp. = approx. 1 medium lemon
Lime	1½ tsp. = approx. 1 medium lime
Orange	1 tsp. =1 medium orange

Pineapple   1 tsp. = approx. ½ cup pineapple
Raspberry   ½ tsp. = approx. ½ cup raspberries
Rum   1 tbsp. = approx. ⅓ cup rum
Strawberry 1 tsp. = approx. ½ cup strawberries

INVENTORY OF INGREDIENTS

Household Honey

Author's term for any mild honey which is suitable for all-purpose day-in-day-out baking and cooking. Try a mild honey like clover, tupelo or willow herb if you aren't yet sure which one your household favors above all.

Skimmed Honey

Half-and-Half Honey

Blended Honey

Mixed Honey

Mixed Molasses

See *Other Homemade Sweeteners* in this section.

Oil

Most supermarket oils are too highly refined and contain objectionable additives. Pick a good all-around cold-pressed unrefined (look for these terms on the label) oil with nothing added. Keep well capped (preferably in a can or dark bottle in the refrigerator). Safflower is best for general baking; use corn oil when you want more flavor.

Baking Soda and Baking Powder

Use these as little as possible. Both contain chemicals that neutralize stomach acidity and interfere with digestion. Choose a baking powder that says "aluminum-free" on label.

Baking Yeast

Most supermarket brands contain objectionable preservatives. Select one that doesn't—from your health food store. Keep refrigerated.

Potassium Chloride

A salt substitute. In view of our heavy salt intake, this is often preferable in recipes. A lot of this can spell trouble too, so be miserly.

Food Yeast

Do not confuse with baking yeast. Also known as Brewer's Yeast, Nutritional Yeast, Eating Yeast. High in protein, minerals and the B vitamin complex. Use as a supplement, stir a tablespoon or two into all your flours. May be eaten as is or used in any prepared foods.

High-Protein Flour

Author's term referring to combinations of the following: wheat germ flour, gluten flour, peanut meal, soybean flour, sunflower meal and triticale, to name a few. Create your own "high-protein flour" by combining ¼ cup each of three of the above plus ¼ cup sifted milk powder.

Baby's Flour

Author's term referring to any flours used singly or in combination from this list: brown rice flour, millet meal, barley flour, soybean flour, oat flour. Categorized this way because they are especially easy to digest and assimilate and are high in protein as well.

Triticale Flour

Made from a special hybrid wheat-rye grain that is 16–20 percent protein. Use up to 50 percent triticale to replace whole wheat flour in recipes (more may result in soggy loaves and baked goods).

Milk Powder

Always use the noninstant type, available at health food stores. Instant varieties are processed by extreme heat which destroys most of the nutrients.

Lactose Powder

Whey Powder

Whey and lactose are rich in B_{12} and the milk sugars which aid in digestion and manufacture of B vitamins in the digestive tract. You might think of them as "powdered yogurt."

Bonemeal

Bonemeal is a relatively tasteless calcium supplement. Add to recipes as you would Food Yeast.

Arrowroot

Use instead of cornstarch (which is highly refined). Arrowroot is easily assimilated by the body, mineral-rich, and does not give a chalky taste to gravies or sauces.

Dried Fruit

Buy unsprayed types at natural food stores. Most super-market dried fruit is sulphured (rather than sun-dried), subjected to artificially fertilized soils, toxic sprays, detergent cleaners and chemical preservatives during the growing and processing.

RECIPES

KIDSTUFF Sweets for Tykes, Babies and Pets

✓ **BUGS' BON-BONS** *(carotene-rich candy without a single unsalutary ingredient)*

½ cup cottage cheese
½ cup cream cheese
   (your own, prefer-
   ably—try the recipe
   on page 39)
⅓ cup peanut butter
   (freshly ground or
   at least unrefined)
2 tbsp. fruit syrup
   #1, 2 or 3
½ tsp. nutmeg

1 tsp. vanilla or pure
   lemon extract
2 tbsp. organic carrot
   syrup (optional)
⅓ cup finely grated
   carrot
toasted wheat germ
   as needed
1 cup soybeans, un-
   salted, toasted and
   coarsely chopped

Blend together all ingredients except the soybeans. This is a messy business best done with the
help of whatever messpots you can round up in your
household. Add as much wheat germ as you need to

produce a dough that is not excessively sticky but not too dry to adhere to the soybeans. Shape little balls (again, with a major assist from the peanut, or rather, soybean gallery), and roll them in the soybeans. Refrigerate before serving.

Makes about two dozen bon-bons.

BASIC BABY'S BREAD *(highly digestible, low in carbohydrate)*

⅓ pound sprouted wheat or rye berries

1⅛ cups scalded milk (unless gummy bread tastes good to you and your cradlebound—that's the sort of bread unscalded milk, with its enzymes still alive and hopping, makes)

2 tbsp. dry baking yeast

2 tbsp. oil (you will get a somewhat chewier bread if this is left out, please note)

1½ tbsp. blackstrap molasses or malt extract

1 tsp. sea salt

2 cups baby flour (brought to room temperature

1½ cups whole wheat flour (also room temperature)

Preheat oven to 350°. Add some of the scalded milk to sprouts and blend to a paste in blender. Pour remaining milk into a large warmed bowl and cover with yeast. Stir in sweetening and, when frothy, blend in everything except whole wheat flour. Knead in whole wheat flour bit by bit until ball of dough is smooth and satiny, as they say. Let rise in a warm spot about 1 hour. Punch down and shape into a small loaf or into baby-shaped buns and let rise another 20 minutes. Grease loaf pans or cookie sheet.

Bake at 350°, 25 minutes for buns, 55–60 minutes for the loaf.

Note: Flour and all bread-making ingredients that aren't at room temperature before being incorporated into the loaf or loafettes to which you aspire will produce soggy results.

See Recycling Note #13

BASIC BABY'S CRACKERBREAD

2½ cups twice-sifted whole wheat flour
2 tbsp. sifted soy flour
2 tbsp. nonfat dry milk powder
2 tbsp. raw wheat germ

3 tbsp. oil or lecithin granules
3 tbsp. household honey or malt extract
1 tsp. vanilla extract

Mix together flours, milk powder and wheat germ. Combine other ingredients and blend them into flours. Knead till you have a ball smooth as (what else?) baby's bottom. Roll on floured board till thin as possible. Cut into bitty baby-sized 1-inch strips.

Bake at 350° on greased cookie sheet for 8 to 10 minutes until browned. Cool thoroughly on cake racks and store in tightly covered containers.

ICHABODS *(a headless handheld sweet)*

⅓ cup soy or dairy butter
1 cup unsulphured molasses or sorghum

½ cup yogurt
¼ cup homemade or date sugar
4 tbsp. food yeast

1 cup unbleached flour	½ tsp. ground cloves
2 cups whole wheat flour	2 tsp. ground ginger
	½ tsp. nutmeg
	½ tsp. salt

Cream butter and molasses. Add yogurt and date sugar. Sift in flours, food yeast and spices. Mix well into a stiff dough. Chill about an hour.

Preheat oven to 350°. Roll out dough on floured board and cut into gingerbread-men shapes. Decapitate (this is where the kids come in) but bake the heads on the same sheet.

Decorate in some befittingly sombre fashion (black sesame seeds? a fudgey coat of carob frosting?) and bake on oiled cookie sheet for about 10 or 12 minutes.

What's Good About It??

Like so many nutritious foods being crowded out of our supermarkets, sorghum is a sort of endangered species among the natural sweeteners, a kind of edible antique-to-be, doubly endearing to those of us who are solidly opposed to the sulphured and oversugared syrups on grocers' shelves. Sorghum ranks next to liver as a source of iron. Your children may turn down the liver, but a sorghum cookie, never. And you don't have to fry it with onions, either.

A CHILD'S COFFEE

Into one cup of plain or fortified hot water put 1 tbsp. blackstrap molasses. Stir, stir, stir. Serve with or without cream.

A CHILD'S CHEESE

Heat 1 quart sweet milk to 110°. Transfer to a large bowl or basin and set in warm spot (oven warmed by pilot light is traditional) for 24 hours. Cheese will have risen to top. Warm oven occasionally during day and stir milk a few times.

Put cheese into wire strainer lined with cheesecloth (yes, this is why they call it that) and allow to drain. A weight on top (maybe a clean doorstop?) will hurry this up. Produces a mozzarella-type cheese that can be sliced.

For green cheese, stir 1 tsp. chlorophyll liquid into cheese before placing in strainer.

A CHILD'S CATSUP (sweet, unspicy and very child-oriented)

2 tbsp. vegetable oil
1 pound fresh tomatoes, in chunks
1 apple, in chunks
1 onion, in chunks
1 onion, chopped finely

½ green pepper, in chunks
¼ cup honey
1 tsp. salt
¼ tsp. cinnamon
¼ cup cider vinegar

Grease a skillet with the vegetable oil. Put in fresh tomatoes, apple and onions, and cook over medium heat until onions are transparent.

Remove from burner and dump into blender. Process at low speed until smooth. Add remaining ingredients. Process till very smooth.

Yields a bit less than one quart.

FUDGESTICKLES

Mix 1 tbsp. carob powder with 5 ounces plain yogurt (plus some honey C powder if you want to fortify further). Spoon into plastic cup, freeze to slush stage, insert sucker stick and freeze again. To eat, simply peel off cup.

CREAMSTICKLES

Cream 1 fresh or drained canned peach in the blender and stir it into 5 ounces of plain yogurt (fortified with honey C, if you wish). Spoon the works into a large paper cup, freeze to slush stage, insert sucker stick and refreeze till ready.

MUNCHKINS *(kiddyfied abbreviated breadsticks)*

1 cup raw wheat germ
½ cup gluten flour
½ cup oat flour (pulverize rolled oats in blender)

1 tbsp. fruit salt (see recipe, page 23)
¾ cup milk or fortified water
5 tbsp. poppy or sesame seeds

Preheat oven to 350°. Combine all ingredients and stir in mixing bowl with fork until you can handle dough well enough to shape and roll. Dough should not be too dry. Knead briefly; break off small pieces of dough (about the size of a lime) and gently shape into fat short cylinders. Roll in seeds and bake about 30 minutes. These taste best on the day of baking (after which they tend to harden somewhat).

Makes about one and a half dozen.

COSTERMONGERS *(caramelized apples)*

1½ cups pure maple
  syrup
½ cup light sweet
  cream
2 tbsp. dairy butter

¾ cup skim milk
  powder (non-
  instant)
6 apples
6 sticks

Mix maple syrup and cream in a large saucepan. Bring mixture to a boil slowly, stirring all the while. If mixture begins to curdle, reduce heat but continue cooking. Cook this simmering mixture to the soft ball stage, stirring often.

Pour into mixing bowl, add butter and cool (about 10 to 15 minutes). Beat in milk powder until the warm sauce will pour very slowly.

Coat each apple by turning it in the caramel sauce. Let excess drip off. Keep a pot of boiling water nearby. If mixture begins to harden or cool too much, set bowl over water until sauce softens again.

Place coated apples on buttered cookie sheet and cool in the refrigerator until caramel hardens.

CORNBALLS

1 part household
  honey
2 parts peanut butter

1 part popcorn flour
  (grind freshly
  popped corn in
  blender)

Combine honey and peanut butter and mix in the popcorn flour until mixture is stiff and manageable. Roll into little balls. Eat raw.

SHAKE UP MUGS *(for the thirsty little mugs about the house)*

Germinated

1 cup warm soy or
  dairy milk
1 tbsp. carob powder
1 tsp. mild salad oil
½ tsp. pure vanilla
  extract

1 tbsp. honey
¼ cup sunflower
  sprouts (alfalfa for a
  second choice)

Put everything into blender and process. Pour into tall slush mug (with a top) or tall glass with an improvised cap, and shake up. Sip with or without straws.

Carbonated

1 quart water
4 tbsp. sassafras or
  sarsaparilla leaves *

½ tsp. bakers' yeast
¼–½ cup household
  honey (according to
  taste)

Heat water and pour over sassafras or sarsaparilla leaves. Let cool until lukewarm, and then stir in bakers' yeast and warm honey.

Let mixture sit, loosely covered, for 12 hours. Chill, pour into slush mugs or glasses (as above), shake till it fizzes and sip with or without cracked ice.

COWABUNGA *(carob yogurt custard)*

2½ cups plain yogurt
½ cup skim milk
  powder

3 medium eggs
¼ cup carob syrup
  (light or dark)

* See Source #1

½ tsp. vanilla extract
5 tbsp. carob powder
pinch of salt and kelp

2 tbsp. food yeast
  (if you want some)
¼ cup carob chips
  (if you have some)

Preheat oven to 325°. Combine milk powder and yogurt thoroughly. Put everything but the carob chips in the blender. Blend at low speed (stopping now and then to help things along with a rubber spatula) until everything is well mixed and mixture is smooth.

Pour into a well-greased ovenproof dish (or individual custard cups, likewise greased) and bake covered for 20 minutes. Uncover and bake 20 more minutes or until firm (watching that top doesn't burn). If desired, toss carob chips on top before last 20 minutes of baking.

COWABUNGA PLUS (carob coating for candy bars)

In a double boiler (or greased saucepan), melt 1 cup of carob chips with 2 tbsp. oil or butter. Quickly coat your candy bars and set to dry. What's left makes a good spread for Instant Cowabunga Toast.

HOMEMADE ROOT BEER (it's the re-al thing)

1 ounce root beer
  extract *
1½ cups honey

1½ tsp. bakers' yeast
  granules
1 cup lukewarm water

Place all ingredients in blender and process at lowest speed until yeast is dissolved. Pour into a gallon jug and add cool water to fill the jug to within an inch of the top. Place lid on *lightly* and

* See Source #8

leave at room temperature for 24 hours. Tighten lid and refrigerate at least 8 hours before serving. On second day after root beer is made, decant into glass juice jars or other such containers. Discard the yeasty residue at jug bottom. This keeps about a week.

What's Good About It??

The statistics on superswilling go like this: The average American (in sickness, health, senility and pubescence) consumes 363 bottles of soda pop a year. The stuff of which such unreal refrigerants are made include: ammoniated glyeyrrhizin, sodiumeta-bisulfite, methylcellulose and eighty other chemical additives. You can make your own: five gallons for about 75¢. What could be more old-fashioned than that?

See Recycling Note #9

PURPLE COW SUPERMILK

1 cup blueberries
1 cup ice water
6 tbsp. noninstant
  milk powder

2 tbsp. household
honey

Blend (in electric blender) until smooth and even.

MAGENTA COW SUPERMILK

Equally dramatic, cheaper and good upholstery for iron-poor blood. Use 2 cups water left from boiling beets, or use beet juice and blend with 6 tbsp. date sugar and 3 or more spoonfuls of milk powder. Blend until frothy and healthily drinkable.

GREEN GOAT SUPERMILK

1 egg yolk
1 cup fresh spinach
   leaves
1 pinch nutmeg

1 cup goat's milk
1 tbsp. honey or date
   sugar

Put yolk into blender and run at low speed, popping spinach leaves one by one through the cap. Add what's left and blend briefly. Good for whatever gets your goat.

CHOCOLATE SPAGHETTI (*quintessential kidstuff*)

2 eggs (or 1 egg and
   1 yolk)
2 tbsp. plain thick
   yogurt or sour
   cream
½ cup sifted carob
   powder
½ cup buckwheat
   flour

1 cup soft whole
   wheat flour
1 tbsp. honey or
   homemade sugar
¼ tsp. salt
1 drop vanilla extract
   (optional)

Put eggs and yogurt in blender, whip and pour into mixing bowl. Stir in everything else and turn out onto a floured board. Knead well (dough should be soft and elastic), adding more flour if needed to counteract stickiness. Chill briefly.

Roll out on floured board until quite thin. Let dry for 15 minutes. Drop into salted boiling water and simmer 8 to 10 minutes. Serve with butter and oil, or the sauce below.

✓ MILK CHOCOLATE SAUCE *(for chocolate spaghetti)*

2 tbsp. butter	1 tbsp. carob powder
1 tbsp. whole wheat flour	½–¾ cups milk
1 tsp. milk powder	1 tsp. lecithin granules

Melt butter and, when bubbly, stir in flour, milk powder and carob powder. Stir over reduced heat until smooth (or you may blend everything in electric blender and then heat). Add warm milk and lecithin granules (this is an emulsifier). Stir until smooth and pour over spaghetti, above, while still warm.

If, being beyond the age of consent, you didn't opt for the foregoing pasta, you can still have the sauce on plain sponge cake, stewed pears or the evening's ice cream, NO?

See Recycling Note #23

✓ DOUGHBOYS *(cut-out cookies of distinction)*

½ cup butter (Why? See Good Earth Bars, page 160)	½ cup finely ground mixed grains (sold as "seven-grain" or "twelve-grain" cereal)
⅓ cup maple sugar (or equal parts date sugar and honey)	2 tsp. double-acting baking powder
1 large egg	½ cup whey powder, milk powder or protein powder
½ cup wheat germ	pinch of salt
½ cup blackstrap molasses or buckwheat honey	1 tsp. coriander
¼ cup milk	
1 cup whole wheat pastry flour	

Stir only enough to mix well. Chill overnight.

Meanwhile, fashion out of heavy cardboard a non-assemblyline-looking doughboy cutter (same general doughy contours as gingerbread men, but in military fashion with arms at sides).

Next day: Roll out dough on pastry cloth about ¼-inch thick. Cut out, running a knife around edges of your homemade cutter, and bake at 350° for about 8 minutes or until brown.

Decorate with candied coriander * or cranberry halves, or pine nuts and blanched raw almonds, for further distinction.

What's Good About It??

A deterrent in the war against White Anglo-Saxon Processed cookies. When they ask you (as they will) about the distinctive flavor, tell them coriander (which they may then tell you is the stuff they use in pomanders, isn't it? It is) is one of the love potion ingredients mentioned in the Arabian Nights and was a spice much loved and liberally used by the Greeks and Egyptians. Nutritionists to-day tell us that if you are careful to get your grains unprocessed with their full complement of germ and bran (as you see here in the making of this cookie) you will enhance the quality of the genes you pass on to your children.

Let Doughboys be much loved and liberally used in your digs.

SUGARLESS ICE CREAM CONES

Bring to a hard boil for about 1 minute:

* *See Source #1*

½ *cup pure maple syrup or ¾ cup maple cream*	¼ *cup butter*

Remove from heat and add:

½ *cup sifted whole wheat flour*	*pinch salt*
⅛ *cup wheat germ or finely ground nutmeats*	1 *cardboard cone dummy*

Preheat oven to 350°. Stir the above ingredients well. When they are well blended, drop a tablespoon at a time onto greased cookie sheet (do one at a time unless you have two uniformed attendants) and bake 6 to 9 minutes or until dough turns maple-sugar color (this time is very variable—don't leave the kitchen). Remove pan from oven. When cookie is slightly cool, remove it with spatula and great care and fold rapidly around the cone dummy, holding in place until cone crisps and holds shape. Quickly remove cone. Cool on rack. Store in airtight cannister.

To make cone dummy: Cut a large triangle out of soft cardboard and roll up into a cone shape. Staple twice.

What's Good About It??

Grocery store gaufrettes were never (are never) like this. If they use more than sixty nonnutritive chemicals in commercial ice cream you can imagine what they're squeezing into the scaffolding. Not so here: pure maple syrup, if you can find and afford it, is probably five times richer in natural minerals than most honeys, although it still doesn't touch blackstrap molasses—which in addition to its minerals has only two-thirds the calories and half the carbohydrates of refined sugar. And should everything not work out copesetically with your cones (some sleight of hand comes in handy at the cone-making stage), abort by crushing and tossing into the granola jar.

Pet Food Division

DOG BISCUITS *(soft pack)*

> 2 eggs *(growing pup-*
> *pies should have*
> *this many a week)*
> 1 cup pitted dates
> *blended smooth*
> *(a good source of*

> *minerals and the*
> *richest natural*
> *source of body fuel)*
> ½ cup shortening
> 2 tbsp. carob powder
> 1 cup bonemeal
> *powder*

Preheat oven to 325°. Put all ingredients in a greased pan and bake about 45 minutes. Biscuits will be soft. Cut into squares.

DOG BISCUITS *(hard pack)*

> 1 tsp. any dry natural
> *sweetener*
> ½ tsp. kelp or sea salt
> 2 cups whole wheat
> *flour*

> 1 cup unbleached
> *white flour*
> 1 cup soy milk
> *powder*
> ⅓ cup shortening
> ½ cup milk

Optional: for liver biscuits, add 2 tbsp. desiccated liver powder.

Preheat oven to 350°. Sift kelp and sweetener with flour. Blend in liver powder, milk powder and shortening. Add just enough milk to make a very stiff dough. Knead on floured board until dough becomes soft and pliable.

Run dough through a meat grinder using coarse blade (or beat steadily with potato masher for 30 minutes until dough blisters, keeping edges turned in). Roll to ½-inch thickness, cut with a biscuit cutter, prick with a fork and bake 30 minutes, at which time the biscuits should be an appropriately lovely bone color.

What's Good About It??

The statutory rape of the sweet tooth has not escaped your hound's tooth. Sugar is a dispensable item in the diet of any dog, yet it appears as the third most frequently compounded ingredient of many canned and "moist" pet foods. So here's a countercultural way to treat your pet. Both biscuits abound in all the essential minerals, especially calcium (thanks to the bonemeal and the soy milk powder). And both are high in the "friendly" carbohydrates which should constitute up to 83 percent of a dog's diet. More woof than nutritional warp, as it were.

Note: These are perfectly palatable for human beings, but for a doggier biscuit you may substitute ½ cup grated turnip and ½ cup cooked peas for the dates. These vegetables supply minerals plus important roughage.

MARESYOATS *(or Doesyoats)*
A sherbety sort of milk for you and your Shetland

1 cup uncooked whole oat groats	2 cups water and 3 cups apple juice
	1 vanilla bean

Wash groats and pressure cook with water and vanilla bean for 45 minutes. (For regular cooking, bring oats and water to a boil, add bean, cover pan, simmer at least 1 hour.) Remove bean and strain. Pour into blender with a half-tray of ice cubes and process till frothy and liquified. Decant into trough and/or tumblers.

Note: Cooked oats may be added to your next muffin batter.

UNPLUGGED BANANAS *(power free plantains for you and your favorite pygmy marmoset; no manmade energy needed to prepare)*

Line up *whole bananas* in their peels *on the hearth* before the fire. Turn once. When skins turn black (about 6 minutes), split them open lengthwise, sprinkle with homemade sugar (see pages 16–18) or Fruit Salt (see page 23) and eat with paw or teaspoon.

CATNIP CHIPS *(a true cat yummy)*

¼ cup flaked dry codfish	¼ tsp. garlic powder
1 cup sifted unbleached white flour	2 tbsp. catnip leaves, crushed
1 tsp. baking powder	½ cup vegetable oil
¼ tsp. salt	4 tbsp. unsulphured molasses

Preheat oven to 375°. Combine flour, codfish, baking powder, seasoning. Cut in shortening until mixture is crumbly. Mix in milk, stirring and kneading until stiff dough forms. Turn out on floured board. Roll out about ⅛-inch thick. With sharp knife cut into little bite-sized squares. Place on greased baking sheet. Sprinkle with catnip leaves (or roll them into dough's surface before cutting out) and bake for about 5 minutes or until browned on bottom. Treat kitty after they've cooled.

BUSHWACKERS (*a sweet unfried sinker for your favorite web-footed friends*)

1 cup whole wheat pastry flour	2 tsp. oil
	2 tsp. sea salt
½ cup millet flour	6 cups boiling water
1 cup apple juice	

Preheat oven to 375°. Mix dry ingredients, add juice and oil and knead thoroughly. Roll into spheres about the size of golf balls and flatten slightly. Make a hole in center of each with your finger. Salt boiling water and drop in donuts a few at a time. When they float to top and are almost doubled in size, remove with slotted spoon. Brush with oil and place on oiled baking sheet. Bake 15–20 minutes or until lightly browned.

Sugaring Off—an intermission

Start here . . .

• Don't go to the zoo without your own zoo food to counter the cotton candy, caramel corn and caffeinated sodas seducing your children from all sides. Edible alternatives to consider: a baggie of date flakes or chips, a sack of homegrown granola, Plum Jerky (see recipe, page 143), Mod-Pods (break up some carob pods into two-inch chunks—remind the kids that the seeds are the disposable part).

• Vermont Toast: Soak two thick slices of homemade bread in pure maple syrup, saturating both sides. Put in a greased skillet and bake in a 375° oven till crispy. Flip once if you like.

• Snap, Crackle, Glop: The sugary part of breakfast feeding began in 1949 with the introduction of sugar-coated flakes. Today, when you buy frosted flakes you pay $1.92 per pound for the sugar.

• To minimize the mucilaginous mess honey makes on your cupboard shelves, set the jar in a pan of soapy water with a small sponge inside. You can wipe the jar after each use and your detergent boat will ward off ants.

• Self-Sweetening "Instant Coffee": Stir one table-spoon blackstrap molasses into a cup of hot water and enjoy a drink richer in calcium than milk, richer than any other food in potassium (which you are probably short on if you are over thirty).

• After-Dinner Mint Substitute absolutely devoid of dextrose: candied mimosa, crystallized coriander or ginger and crystallized mint leaves (see Source #1).

To be continued . . .

VEGETERIA

The Vegetarian Sweet Tooth Is Served: Desserts to Main Dishes

ROSEHIP RELISH

1 cup loose rose hips
1 cup sweet red peppers (fresh, raw, cut up)
splash of rosewater and some rosebuds* (if you're splurging)

3 tbsp. honey
3 tbsp. lemon juice
1 cup dry dates
1 cup dry currants
pinch of mint
½ cup toasted walnuts (for a little nutty-gritty)

Grind everything that's grindable. Add the honey, juice, mint and rosewater. Lovely with cold pork, warm ham, spur-of-the-moment slice of toast.

* See Sources #1 or #10

What's Good About It??

A single cup of pared rose hips may contain as much vitamin C as ten to twelve *dozen* oranges! A tablespoon of this relish a day should be on your agenda. Arab physicians of yore were reputed to cure tuberculosis with rose honey, and rosed honey is still an official remedy in many modern pharmacopoeias. According to the ancient Aristoxenus (320 B.C.), anyone who eats honey, spring onions and bread for his daily breakfast will be free from all diseases throughout his lifetime. You may want to substitute this relish for the onions if it's an antemeridiem repast. A little dab'll do ya.

PICKLED PASCAL & PEARLS (*with homemade honey vinegar*)

2 cups of small pearl or pickling onions	4 quarts boiling water
	4 large garlic cloves
10 (about) medium-sized stalks pascal celery	6 tbsp. honey vinegar (see below)
10 sprays fresh dill-weed	4 small chili peppers (bottled is o.k.)
1 cup coarse (not rock) salt	½ tsp. mustard seed

Parboil onions and cool. Cut celery to the size that suits you and parboil or steam. Cool.

Place both vegetables in a large crock with dillweed. Add salt to boiling water and cool. Add everything else to this water and pour over vegetables. Cover with a cloth, a plate, and a stone to weight it down. Turn every couple of days.

In 10 days to 2 weeks, uncover and cork them up.

HOMEMADE HONEY VINEGAR

Mix 5 parts water with 1 part honey. Boil for 10 minutes in a Pyrex container. Cool and add 1 tsp. bakers' yeast. Put in a wide-mouthed crock or barrel (best of all). Cover with cheesecloth and then lightly with a board or plate. Fermentation will be complete after 4 to 6 weeks. Allow fermentation to continue until taste suits you, then strain through doubled gauze and cap tightly. No refrigeration necessary.

ONIONSKINS *(the compleat vegetarian cracker— skinflint-thin and very slightly sweet)*

1 cup sprouted onion seeds or sprouted rye berries (with root curtailed to ¼ the length of grain— longer ones make soggy baked goods)
4 tbsp. dehydrated onion flakes, ground
1 tbsp. dehydrated vegetable flakes, ground

2 tbsp. vegetable oil
2 egg yolks
1½ cups lima bean flour
½ cup unbleached white flour
pinch sea salt or potassium chloride
1 tbsp. dry malt or malted milk powder
more onion flakes

Grind the sprouts in a food grinder with fine blade and mix with oil, egg yolks, and vegetable flakes which have been ground to a powder by a seed mill or blender. Stir in 1 cup of the combined flours or enough to make a stiff dough. Add dry malt. Knead until smooth and elastic. Cover and let stand on floured board for 15 minutes.

Roll out dough until very thin. Cut into rectangles, rounds, squares or such. Sprinkle top with more onion flakes, pressing them firmly into dough.

Bake in 400° oven for 10 minutes on greased cookie sheet, until lightly browned.

Makes about four dozen smallish crackers.

What's Good About It??

It is no crying matter that onions contain a natural antibiotic substance called allicin which has proven to be an effective agent against the bacteria responsible for fungus infections of the skin, wounds, typhoid and cholera. One mg. of allicin has the potency of twenty-five units of penicillin. Experiments have also shown that "something" in onions increases the enzyme action needed to split up fibrin, the cause of blood clots. Bactericiderata aside, onions contain lots of vitamin C, mostly in their cooked state (cooking softens fibers and releases the vitamin) and the more mature, the less sulphur (should you have difficulty digesting this beneficial veg).

Who would have thought a cracker could be curative?

PICADILLIES

9 *large or 12–15 small*
   cucumbers—un-
   sprayed, unwaxed,
   unchemically
   mucked-with
2 *tbsp. fresh dill,*
   chopped, or 1 tbsp.
   dill seed

⅓ *cup coarse salt*
4 *cups cider vinegar*
2 *cups honey*
1 *cup date sugar*
2 *tbsp. mustard seed*
1 *tbsp. whole cloves*
1 *cinnamon stick*

Carve cucumber into thin slices. (No, don't eviscerate first. The skins and seeds have health-giving properties.) Put into a stone crock or a wide bowl with dillweed. Sprinkle with salt and cover with cold water; let stand overnight.

Drain; rinse with fresh water and drain again.

Combine vinegar, sugar and honey in a large enamelware kettle. Tie spices in a small cloth sack and add. Bring to a boil and cook 5 minutes. Add drained cucumbers and bring to a second boil. Reduce heat and simmer about 20 minutes. Discard spice bag; ladle into hot sterilized pint jars and (if you aren't going to be using these up shortly) process for 5 minutes in a boiling-water bath to seal.

Makes about six pints.

MOOLESS—WITH MOLASSES (a sweet "meat")

½ pound ground pinto beans or sprouted pinto beans
½ medium-sized onion, chopped
1 chili pepper, chopped
1 tbsp. oil
kernels from 2 ears of corn, raw or cooked
½ cup tomatoes, chopped
½ small can tomato paste
1 tbsp. carob powder
1 tbsp. molasses or sorghum
¼ tsp. allspice
1 tsp. herb salt

Soak beans overnight in plenty of water. Drain and grind together with chili pepper and onion. Sauté bean mix in oil for several minutes, lower heat, stir in remaining ingredients and simmer together about 20 minutes. Serve with noodles or toast.

Makes three or four servings.

HAMMY—WITH HONEY

¼ cup millet
1 cup minced cooked
   ham
2 scallions
6 fresh spinach leaves
½ carrot and ½
   celery stalk

1 egg white, whipped
   stiff—add 1 tbsp.
   honey during last
   minute of beating
herb salt and pepper
   or ground dulse

Toast millet over medium heat, stirring all the while. Grind in blender and add to ham. Grind vegetables with ham. Add seasoning. Fold in egg white and shape into small meatballs. Chill.

Steam for 15 minutes. Serve in a soy gravy or cream sauce.

SUGARLESS SUBGUM

1 cup fortified water
   (see page 20)
½ cup date sugar
¼ cup honey or light
   carob syrup
½ cup vinegar
1 cup all together of
   shredded sweet

pickles, with fresh
   shredded green
   pepper and carrot
   (or sweet potato)
   and celery
2 tbsp. arrowroot
   starch
1 tsp. soy sauce

Heat water to boiling. Combine sugar, honey and vinegar and cook until dissolved. Add vegetables and cook 5 minutes. Mix arrowroot and soy sauce well and stir in, cooking until mixture thickens. (If it seems slow in doing this, increase the arrowroot and soy sauce.)

CHINESE HOT SAUCE

2½ cups red chili peppers (or small green frying peppers)

2 cups apricots

1 tbsp. lemon extract (unless you can find preserved lemon—

if so, use 1 tbsp. of that)

1 tbsp. fresh garlic

½ tsp. Chinese Five Spice

5 cups water

Put peppers, apricots, garlic and preserved lemon or extract through meat grinder. Add spice. Cook in water until boiling. Lower heat and let simmer 1½ hours. Pour into sterilized, airtight jar and keep in a warm spot facing sun (if possible) for 3 months. Send out for Chinese food while you're waiting.

COLD COMFORTS Cool, Cold and Frozen Desserts

IRISH MOSS MOUSSE

2 cups milk
¼ ounce Irish moss
(carrageen)*
2–3 strips citrus peel
(lemon, orange,
tangerine), un-
sprayed and washed

4 tbsp. date or home-
made sugar**
4 ounces cream,
whipped
1 egg, separated
blender-chopped
granola for garnish

Prepare a soufflé mold by tying a band of doubled paper around the outside of a mold (should extend about 2 inches above top of mold). Steep moss for 10 to 15 minutes and pick off any discolored parts. Put it in a saucepan with milk and cook until it coats back of spoon. Beat yolk with sugar and strain carrageenan into it. Whisk well until it begins to set. Fold in half the whipped cream and stiffly

* See Source #10
** See Stocking Up

beaten white of egg. Pour into mold (or individual dishes).

When mixture has set, remove paper and garnish with citrus peel, chopped or ground granola or whatever seems most mousse suitable.

What's Good About It??

See "Moss Sauce" (in Remedies) for the good word on Irish moss.

SLUSH PILES (a decarbohydrated dessert)

2 cups grated apples, raw, ripe and sweet

1/4 cup fresh lemon juice

1/2 tsp. ground fennel seed

pinch of salt

4 tbsp. date sugar

3 large egg whites

carob powder (optional)

Combine the first four ingredients with half the sugar. Chill. Meanwhile, beat egg whites until stiff but soft, beat a bit longer with remaining sugar, and then fold them into the apple slush and spoon mixture into small dessert cups. Sprinkle (if that takes your fancy) with carob powder. Chill again.

What's Good About It??

Companionate gardening in any pie or parfait recipe are apples and fennel, according to tradition. Apples without being married to anything else are nutritionally noteworthy as toothbrushes (50 percent more effective than man-made cleaners, claim many dentists), as cholesterol stabilizers (the pectin in them accomplishes that), as agents in hastening the recovery from infections and colds (the malic acid in them is responsible for the latter), and as antiscorbutics, which means they are a good source of vitamin C. And if you'd like to get three times more antiscorbutic than you're getting, switch from MacIntosh apples to Greenings or Northern Spy variety. And don't forget, fennel makes the Slush Pile perfect.

See Recycling Note #18

SELF-SWEETENING SESAME YOGURT

1 cup sesame seeds, hulled and toasted
3 cups fortified water
4 tbsp. whey powder or noninstant skim
milk powder (or increase to 6 tbsp. and omit lactose)
2 tbsp. lactose powder
1 tbsp. fresh yogurt

Grind seeds to a powder in seed mill if you have one; otherwise, grind in blender. Either way, blend the resulting powder with water and blend into a smooth seed milk. Add remaining ingredients and blend again until smooth. Proceed as usual for preparing yogurt or put into yogurt maker and process according to directions.

To satisfy the real sweet tooth, add any natural sweetener after yogurt is finished.

See Recycling Note #11

What's Good About It??

There are presently no federal standards for the composition of cultured sour cream, buttermilk or yogurt. So healthy yogurt is homemade. And even healthier homemade yogurt is made with a super-supplement: sesame seed, 45 percent protein and especially strong in the very amino acids in which milk is weak. If you have no sweet tooth, you may enjoy this plain, since lactose powder is one-sixth as sweet as table sugar.

✓ WONDER WHIP *(a sort of frothy mincemeat)*

1 cup enriched whipped water, lukewarm (see recipe, p. 21)	1 cup fruit (try a fairly economical mixture of minced raisins and currants)
½ cup unrefined vegetable oil	2 egg whites, beaten very stiff
½ cup light carob syrup or acacia honey	¼ tsp. baking powder (aluminum-free)

When water is white and foamy, add next three ingredients to blender jar. Pour mixture over beaten whites (add baking powder after stage of stiffness is reached) and fold in. Spoon into three large parfait glasses or champagne cups. Chill and serve.

What's Good About It??

What's missing? The commercial counterpart of this dessert (do you ingest or inter something made of sugar, corn syrup and ten chemicals?) is undebatably verboten. The virtue of this is that both fruits are rich in blood-building iron (raisins *with* seeds are even higher in this mineral than the havenots), copper, manganese and magnesium. And both (providing you haven't baked, boiled or beaten the life out of them) are celebrated sources of vitamin C, in case anybody turned down his orange juice this morning.

See Recycling Note #19

HERBAL ICE CREAM

2 eggs, separated
⅓ cup pure maple
  syrup
¼ cup regular cream
  or top milk (if raw
  milk is used)

1 cup heavy cream
1 tsp. vanilla
pinch of salt
2 tbsp. Mu tea*
  leaves (or sassafras)

Soak tea leaves in regular cream for ½ hour. Beat egg yolks, and then beat in maple syrup and the regular cream until well blended.

Cook in top of double boiler over hot water until slightly thickened, stirring frequently. After about 20 minutes, remove from heat and chill.

Whip heavy cream until soft peaks form (thick but not stiff). In a second bowl, beat egg whites until stiff but not dry. Mix vanilla and salt with chilled yolk-syrup mixture, and then fold in whipped cream and beaten egg whites. Place in coldest part of freezer to chill for several hours until firm.

Yields about two and a half cups.

What's Good About It??

Ice cream is an old standby that's better stood up unless you can make it yourself. And you can, starting right now. The only thing that might hold you up is the maple syrup; if it isn't the real thing you can scratch that too. (Bringing you right back to those contraband Oreos in the breadbox. Resist.) Real maple syrup is 100 percent syrup and has been produced without formaldehyde sanitizing pellets. (Does that sound any worse than the dry cleaning

---

* Mu tea is a very aromatic anthology of leaves including sassafras available at most health food stores.

fluid, louse killers and paint remover they put in commercial ice creams?) Check your source if you aren't sure about your brand. As for the sassafras, it is said to be a palliative against skin complaints and in its distinctive way makes this ice cream truly a cold comfort.

See Recycling Note #17

MELLOW YELLOW GELATIN

2 six-ounce cans of unsweetened pine-apple juice

6 ounces fortified water

2 tbsp. plain unfla-vored gelatin

½ cup crushed nuts

2 or more tbsp. dried mimosa*

honey (pineapple blossom?)

Heat juice and water to boiling. Dissolve gelatin in ¼ cup cold water and add to juice. Stir well and chill until gelatin starts to jell.

Stir in nuts, add honey to taste, and spoon into parfait glasses. Garnish top of each dessert with mimosa balls.

Chill to serve.

MELON SEED PUDDING *(you have eaten the "outards" of the melon—here's what to do with the innards)*

1 cantaloupe

2 tbsp. orange or pa-paya concentrate or fruit butter

4 tbsp. raw honey

1 tsp. vanilla

1 tbsp. arrowroot starch

2 tbsp. water

* See Source #1

Combine the seeds and pulp of melon with concentrate, honey and vanilla. Blend until smooth. Combine arrowroot with water and add. Blend again.

Cook mixture over medium heat, stirring attentively until thick.

Sprinkle with dried toasted ground melon seeds and serve chilled.

BROWN-AND-SERVE SWEET ROLLS *(biodynamic breakfasting)*

2 tbsp. bakers' yeast
1 cup lukewarm water or juice
1 cup hot water
⅓ cup (more or less) date syrup or maple syrup
¾ cup cold-pressed oil

2 tsp. salt
2 beaten eggs
5 cups whole wheat flour and 1 cup high-protein flour (or 6 cups whole wheat flour)

For filling:

raisins (or currants) or chopped dried dates
chopped seeds or nuts
powdered cinnamon, nutmeg or

Chinese Five Spice
3 tbsp. melted soy butter or oil
3 tbsp. warmed honey or date sugar

For glaze:

3 tbsp. honey and 1 tbsp. water, heated in custard

cup over hot water

Dissolve yeast in warm water or juice and let sit 5 minutes.

Mix hot water, oil, syrup and salt. Beat in eggs and add yeast. Add 2 cups of flour, beating in gradually with electric mixer. Slowly incorporate the rest, switching to wooden spoon. Allow to rise until doubled. Chill.

Separate dough into two balls and roll out into fairly thin rectangles (about 10 inches by 12 inches) and cover with filling (above). Wrap in jelly-roll fashion. Cut into 1-inch slices and place close together on lightly greased cookie sheets. Brush with glaze.

Bake 15 minutes at 400°. Cool. Wrap in foil and put into freezer.

To brown and serve: Place frozen rolls in preheated 400° oven and brown about 15 minutes.

What's Good About It??

Can you get a carrot vitamin out of a dried fruit? Yes. Dates contain significant amounts of vitamin A and B too, and even a relative newcomer to the B complex, mesoinositol. And if you need another reason to buy dates and the syrup made from them, recall that sun-ripening increases the sugar content as much as 30 percent. The high-protein flour here could be a combination such as: wheat germ flour (just powder the flakes in the blender), peanut meal and whole rye flour, plus a little soy flour.

SNOWFLAKES *(a snow-white sweet)*

Take one fresh shelled, drained and peeled coconut* and cut into 2½ inch-wide chunks with a

* *Put a whole coconut in a 400° oven for 15 minutes. Remove and administer a sharp crack with a hammer. Shell will fall away. Trim away dark skin and proceed with the above.*

sharp knife. On a mandoline or similar grater cut chunks into wafer-thin chips, holding the curved side perpendicular to the blade.

Toast chips in a preheated 300° oven for about 50 minutes, tossing them at 10-minute intervals. These keep for weeks in any airtight container.

SNOW CONES

Make some thick cornucopias of heavy butcher paper or lightweight cardboard (or something surpassingly creative), or use homemade sugarless cones (recipe on page 47). Fill a kettle to one-fourth capacity with maple syrup (butter the top edge of the kettle) and heat to boiling, watching the pot carefully. When thermometer reads 230°, remove one tablespoonful and cool slightly over snow or crushed ice. If poured syrup clings to a fork like soft taffy, batch is ready.

Cool boiling liquid to between 150° and 190°. Heap clean new snow into cones and pour a bit of syrup into each.

Remember that maple syrup will lose about one-fifth its volume in the boiling, when deciding how much you will need.

FREEZEBURGER #1

Put ¼ cup of seeds, ¼ cup milk or fortified water, 1 egg yolk and a few dates, raisins or figs into blender. When liquified, pour into saucer or foil potato boat and freeze. Take out of freezer 15 to 20 minutes before serving.

FREEZEBURGER #2

Mash 2 very ripe bananas with fruit butter to taste. Form into patties and dredge with unsweetened coconut. Freeze in individual baggies and take out of freezer 15 to 20 minutes before hunger strikes.

FREEZEBURGER #3

Put 1 cup hot water in blender and add 2 tbsp. gelatin. Let foam up and melt in. Add ¼ cup household honey, ¼ cup oil, and ½ tsp. vanilla. Drop in ice cubes until liquid thickens and won't incorporate any more cubes. Spoon out into patties on greased freezer paper and freeze—remove 15 to 20 minutes before they are needed.

HASTY PUDDING (a raw and restorative stirabout in a glass)

2 cups unsulphured sun-dried fruit, finely chopped or ground (start with apricots and then add figs, prunes, or raisins, bananas, apples, etc.—whatever combination seems congruent to you)

2 cups plain yogurt (homemade is best because it's thicker)

Turn the fruit into mincemeat using an electric food mill (first choice for those who would like to avoid athletic contests in the kitchen), hand-meatgrinder, or electric blender (here, be sure to introduce fruits already chopped, slowly and gradually). Combine fruit with yogurt by hand or re-blend in blender.

Pour into tumblers, parfait glasses or cups and chill. Or eat on the spot.

Note: If you're using week-old yogurt, a bit of light honey (clover or orange blossom) may be needed.

What's Good About It??

Even if you're all thumbs, this is five-minute foodmaking at its foolproof finest. Nutritionally superior to commercial puddings because it's uncooked and therefore provides the full benefit of all the enzymes and, assuming you've used apricots, the vitamins and minerals, which are (reading from left to right): A, B, C (four times more than oranges), thiamine, iron and copper. And thanks to the yogurt, your intestinal absorption of calcium will be doubled. (Add the figs for superior calcium benefits.) Remember this one when you have the breakfast blahs.

Sugaring Off—an intermission

read on

• In the last 150 years there has been a fifty-fold increase in world sugar production. The sugar industry presently sells slightly under 2½ billion tons of sugar to the American public.

• Toasting dextrinizes (sweetens) bread, but it also destroys vitamin B_1.

• Bad Mouthing: The average American has five unfilled cavities. (National Institute of Dental Research.)

• Appetite Depressant: Cut a sweet potato widthwise and pare off paper-thin slices with a potato peeler. Place on greased cookie sheet and bake 20 minutes at 400°. Sprinkle with any homemade sugar or date sugar (see Stocking Up).

• Pot Roast Rub: Combine 1 tbsp. maple sugar with ¼ cup flour and 1 tsp. each salt, poultry seasoning and dry mustard. Rub all sides of pot roast. Brown meat as usual and proceed according to your customary recipe.

• In 1971 the advertising budgets of both Coca-Cola and Pepsi Cola were larger than the entire budget of the Food and Drug Administration's Bureau of Foods. (*Nutrition Scoreboard*, Michael Jacobsen.)

• Taffy Toast (or Vermont Toast II): Combine ¼ cup molasses, ¼ cup honey and ¼ cup oil in a heat-proof jar. Warm in hot water and pour over 3 man-sized slices of homemade whole-grain bread lining bottom of a large, lightly oiled skillet. Bake in 350° oven about 15 minutes. Pour any remaining pan juices over toast and wash skillet immediately.

To be continued . . .

EITHER/OR FOODS
Adventures in Two-Way Sweets

BABY'S FORMULA (*or Thickshake for a Mama-To-Be*)

1 quart whole milk or homemade whole-milk yogurt

⅔ cup boiled calcium cooking water or fortified water, cooled

3–5 tbsp. lactose

2 tbsp. powdered whey or calcium powder

¼ tsp. magnesium oxide or Epsom salts

½ tsp. liquid vitamin C or rose hip powder

1 tsp. nutritional yeast

¼ tsp. granular kelp

½ tsp. cold-pressed salad oil

1 tsp. lecithin granules or flakes

If yogurt is not used, add: 1–4 tbsp. plain yogurt

For formula: Combine all ingredients in pitcher

or blender and mix well. Fill bottles immediately or keep in refrigerator until needed.

For thickshake: Add ¼ cup milk powder and 1 egg yolk beaten with 3 tbsp. honey. Combine all ingredients in blender and mix well.

What's Good About It??

Yogurt-formula babies (like breast-fed infants) have fewer intestinal troubles and respiratory complaints, and a yogurt formula need not be sterilized. As for you, consider the fact that cultured yogurt is higher in folic acid (something a mother-to-be is bound to run short on) than other milk products. As a matter of fact, the nutritional value of the milk protein itself increases considerably during yogurt-making. And after you've added milk powder, you have an ingredient that is 36.5 percent protein (lean beef is 19.7 percent), 8 percent minerals (most foods have only 1 percent), and is rich in the vitamin B complex. (And did you know the Egyptians were the first to sun-dry milk? Tut-tut, it's true.)

See Recycling Note #5

SUGAR-FREE PROTEIN DRINK (*either a quick breakfast or lunch . . . or, a Dem Som for One*)

1 cup enriched water
2 tbsp. toasted sesame or sunflower seeds
2 tbsp. of a non-blatant low-levulose honey like clover or alfalfa (or more, if your sweet tooth is hyperactive)

¼ cup whey powder or milk powder
2 tbsp. roasted peanut meal (2 tbsp. peanut butter is okay too)
2 tbsp. soy lecithin granules
1 tbsp. food yeast

Combine first three ingredients in blender and process. Now you have a "nut milk." To this add what remains and blend again. Gut issue of the goodest sort.

What's Good About It??

You should start the day with twenty grams of protein—that's four and a half tablespoons peanut butter, but why walk around with the morning's Recommended Daily Allowance of protein stuck to the roof of your mouth? This is a better way to come by both protein and peanuts. And make the lecithin a nonoptional ingredient. It's brain food, so save a dab for baby, too. (Did you know that the brain is 80 percent matured by the age of three?) Drink up and put a tiger in your think tank.

See Recycling Note #22

✓ **CRUNCHY CRITTERS** *(escape eating by-the-each; chippery from the kettle or the griddle)*

2 tbsp. shortening (no, not lard)	2 tsp. salt
2 cups ungerminated cornmeal, blended with ¼ cup chia seeds and 1¼ cups unbleached flour	1 cup fortified water or sweet stock
	1 tbsp. maple syrup or molasses
	oil for deep-frying
	whey, arrowroot or
1 tsp. baking powder	skim milk powder

Griddle Critters: Cut shortening into flours and salt. Add water and stir into ball. Turn out onto board floured with cornmeal and knead a bit. Shape into balls (golf-ball size) and allow to rest while you heat griddle.

Roll balls out to ¼-inch thickness and brown both sides on the griddle till crispy brown. Eat as is—which is pretty good. Or dip into skimmed honey.

Kettle Critters: Follow instructions above but, after shaping, roll dough balls out thinner than pie crust. Cut out large circles or rectangles and fry quickly in hot oil (½ inch deep in skillet), drain, and dredge in mock confectioner's coating (arrowroot, whey or dry milk powder).

What's Good About It??

More than 80 percent of the 8,000 food items sold in grocery stores are convenience foods. And a constant in convenience foods is hydrogenated oil, which is to be avoided. Why? Because the molecular modification of oil by refining changes some of the desirable fatty acids to less desirable ones, and some are converted into unnatural forms. The new ones don't act in the same way as the natural ones; they may be harmful to your health, so homemake your chips.

BOGUS BANANA BREAD*(. . . or Phony Parsnip Cake)*

For bread:

3 *pounds bogus bananas (parsnips)*	1 *tsp. vanilla extract*
2 *tbsp. sesame oil*	1 *lemon*
1 *tsp. sea salt*	1½ *cups bulgur or cracked wheat*
4 *cups apple juice*	¼ *cup nut butter*

For cake:

3 *pounds phoney*   *Plus all of the ingre-*
   parsnips (bananas)   *dients above except*
2 *egg whites, beaten*   *parsnips (decrease*
                                  juice to 2 cups)

For bread: Preheat oven to 375°. Scrub parsnips and slice into thin rounds. Heat oil in pressure cooker or large skillet and sauté parsnips for 10 minutes. Add salt and 1 cup apple juice. Cover and cook 45 minutes (or cook under medium pressure for 20 minutes). Puree parsnips. Add remaining apple juice to puree, and simmer in covered pan for 10 minutes. Add grated lemon peel and lemon juice. Sauté bulgur in sesame oil and steam in covered skillet for 15 minutes. Add this to puree along with nut butter. Pour into oiled loaf pan and bake 1 hour.

For cake: Grate lemon rind and add with lemon juice to mashed bananas. Add extract. Sauté bulgur in oil, add apple juice and simmer 15 minutes in covered skillet. Combine this with mashed banana. Stir in nut butter and fold in egg whites. Bake 1 hour at 375° in greased heatproof casserole dish.

What's Good About It??

If your kids can always tell a carrot when it's coming—try them on the carrot's cousin, the parsnip. Parsnips, when cooked and cooked and cooked, become quite sweet and develop an uncanny resemblance in both taste and texture to bananas, so you can interchange them in recipes like these. The parsnip is a charming and unjustly ignored underground (it's a root veg, yes) food. Rich in potassium (like bananas), it has lots of B_1 and C. It makes a very good addition at any point of a meal heavy in starches or protein.

TWO TEA-LEAF MARINADES . . . or *Spicy Salad Dressings*

#1

2 cups boiling water
4 tbsp. ginseng tea
  leaves
½ cup mild apple
  cider or honey
  vinegar
¼ cup mixed honey

bouquet garni: 1 pinch
each Chinese Five
Spice, peppercorns,
½ cinnamon stick,
mustard seeds, in a
cheesecloth bag

Combine water and tea leaves and let steep 10 minutes. Add cider and honey and bouquet garni (if you're fresh out of cheesecloth, try using a large gauze pad from the medicine cabinet). Bring to a boil and simmer 20 minutes. (Now's the time to steam-cook whatever it is you're going to marinate —it's good for pickling squares of To-Fu or slices of turnip or hard-boiled eggs.)

Let marinade cool for a day (with the vegetables, eggs, whatever in it) so flavors can marry. Boil down marinade by half and serve over vegetables.

#2

2 cups of freshly
  brewed alfalfa leaf
  tea
the used tea leaves
¼ cup vinegar
4 tbsp. date sugar

bouquet garni:
1 crushed clove, ½
tsp. each of cumin
seed, celery seed,
fennel seed

Bring everything to a boil and simmer for 20

minutes. Meanwhile, cook (preferably in the steamer) some string-free celery sticks, sliced fresh fennel or rutabaga, thick spears of parsnip. Add these vegetables to the marinade and let it cool in refrigerator for a day (ideally). Or boil and reduce liquid by half to serve hot over vegetables.

See Recycling Note #25

PUFF'N'STUFF *(stuff to stuff stuff with—or a meatless side dish)*

1 pound raw chestnuts
1 cup cooked bulgur
1 cup grated raw winter squash or sweet potato
2 tbsp. butter
1 cup crumbs (cake, sweetbread, cupcake, gingerbread remains)

2 eggs, beaten
1 tsp. Chinese Five Spice or pumpkinpie spice
2–3 tbsp. homemade light-brown or dryroasted "sugar"
¼ cup currants or chopped raisins
diluted fruit juice, as needed

Boil chestnuts 45 minutes or until tender. Remove shell and inner skin while still hot. Use nut grinder, food chopper or knife to grind nutmeats and mix them with cooked bulgur. (Use 1 cup grain to 1½ cups water and steam 15 minutes, or till fluffy.) Sauté shredded squash in butter, add cake crumbs, sauté, and turn into bowl, adding all other ingredients. Add a small amount of very diluted fruit juice if more moisture is necessary.

This is a pungent dressing to stuff whole fish with, or celery stalks, or thin pancakes, or whatever aching edible voids you are faced with.

What's Good About It??

One-third of all meals in America are eaten out. If this is happening in your household, here's something to keep them home at night. Bulgur, a more convenient substitute for rice, is partially precooked but retains the nutrients of the germ and the bran. And if nobody's encountered a chestnut around your place lately, change all that, too. Chestnuts supply fine-quality protein and are free from meat's uric acid. But if you're watching carbohydrates (these are very high), this is Puff'n'stuff to stuff someone else with.

FOCCACIO FOR HEALTH *(could be a flatbread, could be sweet pizza)*

½ cup warm water or whey
1 tbsp. bakers' yeast
1 cup whole wheat flour
2–3 tbsp. apricot kernel (or sesame seed) oil
2 tbsp. honey

½ cup chia or alfalfa sprouts, coarsely chopped
½ tsp. salt
½ tsp. anise seed, freshly ground (if possible)
fruit salt (see page 23)

Preheat oven to 400°. Dissolve yeast in water for 5 minutes. Add half the flour, the honey and 1 tbsp. oil. Turn out on floured board and knead in sprouts, salt and anise and remaining flour. When smooth, roll out into a round about 10 inches in diameter (if that is the size of your skillet). Grease the inside of a 10-inch cast-iron skillet and pat dough snugly inside. Make depressions every inch or so with your finger, sprinkle with remaining oil and fruit salt (cinnamon, too, if you like), and put into a 400° oven for 25 minutes.

Cut into strips or wedges. Serve hot.

What's Good About It??

Did you know that under government regulations, the ingredients of white, whole wheat and raisin breads need not be disclosed? Another reason why you're baking your own bread today. And if you're inclined to think of the alfalfa sprouts as an either/or ingredient, consider the fact that their detoxification properties surpass all other foods, that they have ten times the mineral value of most grains, and that they contain more vitamin C than almost any available foodstuff. As for the apricot kernel oil, not only does it taste good, but it's a very rich source of vitamin B_{17}, a vitamin most of us (unless we are grass-munching vegetarians) are probably deficient in.

COWLESS ICE CREAM . . . or *Cowless Collins*
(*with Cowless Cherries*)

⅓ *cup blossom honey or semi-sorghum*
½ *cup soy milk powder*
1 *cup of sesame cream (blend 1 cup sesame seeds with 1 cup water and 1 tsp. honey)*
1 *cup nut milk (1 cup fortified water*

blended with ¼ cup nuts or nut meal)
2 *egg yolks*
1 *tbsp. cherry concentrate*
and of course, if you have them, 1 or more cups fresh cherries

Beat everything until smooth. Pour into ice cube trays and freeze until solidified. Serve in sugarless cones (recipe on page 47). Or forget freezing—just pour into Tom Collins glasses and tipple on the spot.

See Recycling Note #10

What's Good About It??

Does it cheer you to hear that the cherry flavor in commercial cherry ice cream is an inflammable liquid called aldehyde C17, also used in making aniline dyes, plastics and rubber? Real cherries (and the concentrate that comes from them) are a good source of vitamin A and are among the very best sources of three blood-building minerals: copper, iron and manganese. Another thing your ice cream will contain that theirs won't is a goodly supply of nonanimal calcium. Did you know sesame milk has more calcium than cow's milk? Almost three times as much, and without the fat that stores DDT so effectively. And it's a valuable aid in counteracting cholesterol buildup in the blood (because of its calcium and lecithin content). Dairyless and delicious.

BAKE OFFS Upbeat Eating Out of Your Oven

DOUBLE WHAMMIES *(date-filled cookies)*

Cookie:

½ cup light-bodied honey (clover would be a good choice)
½ cup cold-pressed cooking oil
¾ cup date syrup
1 large egg
juice and rind of ¼ organic lemon

3 cups whole wheat flour, or half whole wheat and half unbleached white
1 tsp. baking powder (aluminum-free)
½ tsp. salt

Filling:

2 cups ground dates
½ cup honey

⅛ cup water
juice of ½ lemon

Preheat oven to 400°. Cream honey, oil and

syrup. Add beaten eggs, lemon juice and rind. Sift flour with baking powder and salt and add to rest of ingredients.

Roll dough quite thin; cut into strips about 6 inches long and 3 inches wide. Put filling (see below) in center of strip and lap sides over.

Bake 15 minutes at 400°. Cool. Cut into desired size crosswise, then make an indentation in the center of the cookie with a dull knife, creating "Double Whammies."

Filling: Combine all filling ingredients in a saucepan and cook 15 minutes, stirring constantly. Cool.

What's Good About It??

If it was good enough for Tutankhamen, it should be good enough for you. Besides being one of the oldest fruits known to man, the date is the finest natural source of sugar (and therefore energy) known. It is highly alkalizing and a rich repository of minerals like iron, magnesium and potassium.

If you take a ten-minute swim, you can just about pay off the caloric toll you chalk up by tossing off two of these lovely things. Running is a good bet too, about six very vigorous minutes' worth—or stick to a single Whammy.

HONEY BUNS (*crunchy, pungent, homey*)

1 cup milk
2 tbsp. bakers' yeast
½ stick butter
½ cup orange blossom honey
¼ cup orange juice concentrate

1½ cups coarse rye flour (grind the berries in your coffee grinder or blender if the traffic will bear)

1½ cups coarse whole
  wheat (grind your
  own, as above)
1 cup gluten flour
2 eggs, beaten

½ to 1 cup un-
  bleached white
  flour
shredded orange peel
  (organic)

Heat ¼ cup milk to approximately 105°. Dissolve yeast. Scald remaining milk and add butter. Allow to melt with saucepan cover on. Cool to lukewarm and add, with honey, to yeast. Stir and let rest 15 minutes.

Add juice. Freshly coarse-ground rye and wheat is incomparable (tastes better, smells nicer and gives better texture to the dough, plus the nutritional benefits). Add this next if you can, the storebought preground stuff if you must, along with the gluten flour. Start with 2 or 3 cups and beat with electric mixer until smooth. Then add eggs, and finish beating in remaining flour by hand. Add peel.

Turn dough out on floured board and knead about 10 minutes until smooth and elastic. Put in greased bowl and let rise 1 hour.

Divide dough into lots and lots of little balls and place on greased cookie sheets. Make a cross depression (as you would for soda bread) atop each bun and cover the sheets with tea towels. Allow to rise 30 minutes. Preheat oven to 375°.

Bake about 10 minutes under foil. Remove, brush tops with milk or beaten egg and bake 10 minutes more (or until golden brown).

Serve liberally slathered with butter and honey. Makes two dozen.

What's Good About It??

Tired? A low alkali reserve often means chronic fatigue. Solution? Honey, a highly alkaline food that's a famous foe of fatigue. Excepting the date, there is no natural food that surpasses it as a source of heat and energy. And it's six times richer in fuel value than milk. So when you're having your sixth honey bun of the day, store this little speech away.

For gift-giving (to those who would also like to be transported to the land of milk and honey if only for the brief length of a bun): Bake dough balls (making them much larger) in small buttered soufflé dishes (one bun to a dish). Adjust oven time (an additional five to ten minutes will be necessary). After cooking, launder dishes, cool bread and repack in the dishes. Wrap the whole lot and beribbon.

UPPER CRUSTS

Coconut-Flavored

1 cup wheat germ	¼ cup oil
⅓ cup coconut shreds	2 tbsp. honey
¼ tsp. salt	

Stir dry ingredients together. Mix in oil and honey and stir well. Roll out between two pieces of wax paper. Bake as top crust of deep dish pie (at 350° for length of time recipe specifies).

Walnut-Flavored

¾ cup ground walnuts	2 tbsp. oil
½ cup flour	2 tbsp. honey

Proceed according to directions above.

HALF-BAKED COOKIES

2 cups soy milk
powder

1 cup skim milk pow-
der plus 1 cup
powdered whey (or
2 cups of one or the
other)

honey-carob syrup
(your own or the
commercial kind

which includes ar-
rowroot starch and
vanilla flavoring)

vanilla or almond ex-
tract (omit if using
a storebought syrup)

¼ cup granola or
chopped nuts

¼ cup or more ar-
rowroot starch

Carob Frosting:

¼ cup sifted carob
powder

honey and water as
needed for icing
consistency

Combine the milk powders in a large bowl and blend in enough syrup to make a satiny, slightly sticky but still manageable dough. Add flavoring, if used. Stir in nuts or granola. Shape into "fingers" and roll in arrowroot. Place on oiled and floured cookie sheet. Paint with carob frosting.

Put into 350° oven and bake only until half done (about 5 to 7 minutes).

What's Good About It??

Don't tell your children but these cookies aren't even half bad for them, unlike most of the sugary concoctions in hand-to-hand circulation these days. Not only is whey our greatest sodium food, but it contains most of the B and other water-soluble vitamins that are lost when milk is turned into cheese.

See, a bit of dietary disestablishmentarianism (cookies without oil, or flour, or eggs) never hurt anybody.

SPUDNUTS

(You've got to have something to put under the sugarless doughnut glaze on page 134, don't you?)

½ cup milk
½ cup fresh sweet potato, chopped (skin too, if not sprayed)
½ cup sour cream
2 tbsp. butter
2 tsp. any natural sweetener (consider organic carrot syrup or papaya concentrate)
1 cake compressed yeast

3 egg yolks (What about the whites? *)
½ tsp. salt
1 tsp. allspice
½ ounce raw sweet potato, finely grated
2 cups whole wheat flour plus ½ cup unbleached white flour
cooking oil (not the good stuff)

Cook potato in milk until tender. Put through sieve; if you have less than ½ cup, add milk to make that measure. Add sour cream and scald this combination. Add butter and sweetener and wait until mixture is lukewarm.

Crumble and stir in yeast until dissolved. Add yolks and salt. Beat in allspice, sweet potato and flours. Dough will be soft. Put into refrigerator or leave in kitchen. Punch down in about an hour (or when light).

Roll dough to ½-inch thickness. Cut with doughnut cutter (or two water glasses—one small, one

* See recipe for Cocoa Puffs, page 107.

large) and set on bread board, covered, for 5 minutes.

Deep-fry a few at a time in fresh non-special oil heated to 375°. Drain on paper toweling. When cooled, paste on that glaze on page 134.

COMPLETE FLOP

(A sort of flip-flop fat pancake with the complete protein of coconut as the star ingredient)

Topping (or bottoming, if you prefer):

6 tbsp. butter	½ cup date sugar
thin slice fresh ginger (optional)	1½ cups shredded coconut, unsweetened

Batter:

1½ cups whole wheat pastry flour	¼ cup light-brown sugar
2½ tsp. baking powder (aluminum-free)	½ tsp. ginger
	1 tsp. pure vanilla
½ tsp. salt	1 egg plus 1 yolk, well beaten
½ cup butter	½ cup coconut or dairy milk
½ cup honey	

For topping: Melt butter in a flat-bottomed 8-inch iron skillet. Sauté ginger slice, remove, add sugar and coconut and stir until combined. Remove from heat.

For batter: Preheat oven to 350°. Sift flour, baking powder and salt three times (for lighter end results). Cream butter, honey, sugar, ginger, eggs and vanilla. Mix half of creamed mixture into dry ingredients, then half of the milk. Repeat this step.

But do not overmix. Pour batter on top of coconut topping in skillet. Bake at 350° for about 35 minutes.

Remove from oven, loosen sides with spatula. Immediately flip-flop onto a waiting cake platter.

What's Good About It??

Coconut, unlike many another nut, is a complete protein—which means that it contains all of the essential amino acids (which is more than you can say for a T-bone steak). And what else it has in abundance is potassium, phosphorus, magnesium and even a bit of iodine. It's a very fine food for babies since it is readily assimilated by the body without much intestinal hocus-pocus (just like honey) and has a mild peptic action on the stomach (which is again more than you can say for a T-bone steak). A vital vittle.

See Recycling Note #8

RUBBER BABY BUGGY BUMPERS (*a beguiling, bagelish, moderately sweet small bread*)

2 tbsp. bakers' yeast	⅛ cup oil
¾ cup lukewarm potato water *	2 eggs, lightly beaten
3 cups of triticale or whole wheat flour	1 or 2 ounces crushed seeds (chia, flax, sesame, poppy, whatever)
1 cup gluten flour	1 quart boiling water
½ tsp. salt	
¼ cup honey	

Dissolve the yeast in half the potato water and stir into the sifted flours. Combine honey, oil, salt

* *Boil a small chopped potato until soft, drain and sieve some of potato into cooking water.*

and remaining potato water. Stir into flour mixture. Add eggs and beat to form a dough.

Knead for 10 minutes on a floured board. Add more flour if dough is not quite firm. Knead in half the seeds.

Put dough in a buttered bowl, cover, and let rise at room temperature until doubled in bulk (1½ to 2 hours).

Preheat oven to 450°. Knead dough again until smooth and rubbery. Pinch off small wads of dough and roll into ropes 3 or 4 inches long. Bring ends of dough together in a doughnut shape and press in some more crushed seeds. Drop about three baby bumpers at a time into pot of boiling water, turning them over as they rise to the top. Boil 1 minute.

Place on greased cookie sheet and bake until golden brown, about 6 to 8 minutes.

Makes about thirty.

PETIT PATE A CHOUX *(little noncariogenic cream puffs)*

Puffs:

2 tbsp. cornstarch	1 cup cold water
½ cup rye flour	½ tsp. salt
½ cup cold-pressed oil	4 eggs

Preheat oven to 400°. Mix cornstarch with flour. Combine oil, cold water and salt in saucepan. Bring to a boil over medium heat. Remove from burner and turn heat to low. Add flour mixture all at once, beating constantly until the two mixtures are incorporated. Return saucepan to heat and continue beating until mixture is smooth and forms a ball (a minute or two).

Transfer mixture to mixing bowl and cool slightly. Add eggs, one at a time, beating well after each. (Use electric mixer for best results.) Continue beating until mixture is smooth and glossy.

Drop by modest tablespoonfuls on ungreased cookie sheet. Bake 30 minutes, until puffy and browned. Turn off oven and let puffs remain therein another 10 minutes. Remove and cool on wire rack.

To serve, cut off tops of puffs with sharp knife and remove any soft dough inside. Spoon in cream filling just before serving and replace top.

Cream filling:

½ cup instant milk powder	1 tbsp. dry malt sweetener or 3 tbsp. honey
½ cup ice water	
1 tbsp. lemon juice	

Chill a 2-cup measuring cup, the beaters from your mixer, and the instant powdered milk. Pour the ice water into this and beat until stiff. Add lemon juice and sweetener and beat again. Chill until ready to use.

SORGHUM SNAPS *(Glorioski, a genuine gingersnap!)*

¼ cup oil	sure consumers of this cookie know it.)
1 cup sorghum	
1 egg	4 tsp. ginger
½ tsp. lemon extract	¼ cup lecithin granules (these replace ¼ of the oil ordinarily used in recipes like this)
pinch or two of lemongrass (A circumstantial ingredient, what else? But nice. If you use it, make	

4 cups sifted whole
   wheat flour
½ cup wheat germ
1 tsp. baking powder

½ tsp. salt
⅛ cup chopped
   pistachio nuts

Blend oil, sorghum, egg, extract, lemongrass. Heat gently. Sift dry ingredients and add to first mixture. Blend in nuts and wrap dough in wax paper. Chill.

Roll out dough till wafer thin (a small ball at a time) on floured board, and cut with a cookie cutter. For a sparkly effect, sprinkle with plain gelatin rather than sugar.

Bake on greased sheet at 375° for 12 to 15 minutes.

What's Good About It??

There's a blood relationship, so to speak, between sorghum and pistachio nuts, since they both contain goodly amounts of the blood-building mineral, iron. To boot, the pistachios contain higher concentrations of potassium than most nuts, whereas sorghum provides twice as much calcium as maple syrup (which you could use here, if that's what the pantry holds instead). All around, for a cookie, this is snappy stuff.

WASPS: WHITE ANGLO SAXON PROTEST COOKIES (no white sugar or white flour; a sort of sugarless sugar cookie)

Cookies:

½ cup butter, or ¼
   cup butter and ¼
   cup oil

½ cup coconut,
   finely powdered in
   blender

¼ cup white sesame
seeds, powdered

2 eggs

2 cups rice polish or
rice flour

¾ cups barley flour
or unbleached white
flour

2 tsp. baking powder
(aluminum-free)

1 tsp. flavoring extract

Cream butter with coconut and sesame seeds. Beat in eggs and add dry ingredients. Or you can omit the baking powder and separate eggs, adding the beaten whites last. Add flavoring extract. Chill dough 3 to 4 hours.

Preheat oven to 375°. Roll out dough fairly thin and cut into desired shapes. If there are no shapes you wish to cut the dough into, you may protest this too, and simply use a water glass.

Bake for about 7 minutes, perhaps longer. Apply icing (below) while cookies are still warm.

WASP icing:

1 egg white
1 tbsp. honey
1 tbsp. milk powder

1 tbsp. arrowroot
starch

Whip egg white at room temperature until nearly stiff. Dribble in warm honey and whip some more. Fold in milk powder and arrowroot. Beat until meringuey, increasing the arrowroot if further stiffness is wanted.

See Recycling Note #7

WAFFLE COOKIES *(an unrefined celebration for unrefined small folk)*

1 cup whole wheat pastry flour	1 cup yogurt cream (or sour cream) *
1 tsp. salt	5 tbsp. light or dark brown homemade sugar **
¼ cup soy flour	
2 tsp. baking powder	
2 eggs, separated	½ cup chopped nuts (your choice)
3 tbsp. oil or melted butter	

Stir dry ingredients together. Beat yolks; add butter, sour cream and sugar. Stir into dry ingredients. Beat egg whites until stiff and fold into batter. Fold in nuts. Ladle batter onto hot oiled waffle-iron, by tablespoons. Good hot or lukewarm. Good with that doughnut glaze (page 134) too.

What's Good About It??

It's been reported that eight ounces of yogurt has an antibiotic value of fourteen units of penicillin. You won't find preventative medicine like that in storebought cookies. Unlikely that you'd find a half-cup of sunflower seeds there, either, so why not try them here because, surprisingly enough, they are a richer source of iron than raisins. Or if you're low on calcium, almonds (one cupful) beat cow's milk (one glass) all hollow.

Wonderful waffles, either way.

* *Drain 1¼ cups of yogurt in a cheesecloth-lined strainer overnight. Result will be a thick yogurt sour cream. Drippings are whey.*

** *See Stocking Up*

PRESSURE COOKER CAKE *(cake-baking by aquaculture?)*

2 cups buttermilk (or thinned yogurt)
¾ cup molasses
1 tsp. salt
1 tsp. allspice
¼ cup homemade sugar
1 cup whole wheat flour
1 cup high protein flour
2 cups undegerminated cornmeal
2 whipped egg whites
hot water

Mix milk and molasses. Add salt, spice and sugar and beat in the flours and meal. Fold in egg whites. Transfer batter to two well-greased coffee cans. Tie two thicknesses of wax paper over tops. Place on rack in pressure cooker and pour in enough hot or boiling water to come halfway up the cans. Close cooker.

Presteam for 30 minutes. Bring pressure to 15 pounds and process for 40 minutes more. Cool slightly, loosen with rubber spatula and remove. When cooled, spread with Rice Icing (recipe on page 132) or the following:

SIMPLE HONEY SYRUP

Boil 1 cup of honey with 1 cup water until it reaches the consistency of a thick syrup. Use this topping while the cake is still oven-warm.

FOODCHOPPER FLAPJACKS *(a life preserver for that kitchen factotum, your electric blender)*

4 dates, figs or prunes
1 firm apple, organic (so you can use the peel too), cored and stemmed

4 Brazil and/or hickory nuts	2 eggs
2 large slices oven-dried bread (3 if not homemade)	½ tsp. baking powder (aluminum-free), optional

Put fruits, nuts and bread through food grinder. Handbeat eggs and add them to ground mixture. Add baking powder and, if batter is too thick, thin out with yogurt. Cook on prepared hot griddle and serve with warmed apple blossom honey or date syrup.

What's Good About It??

A six-year survey conducted by Pennsylvania State University has found that only one person in 1,000 escapes malnutrition, despite the fact that we eat 1,500 pounds of food a year. Another fact: One ounce of extra fat will take two to seven days off your life. This works out to 43.2 days per pound. So there's something lifesaving, all right, about a good breakfast with natural foods that stave off hidden hungers—natural foods like Brazil nuts, which are very rich indeed in fat, starch and protein that should keep you unhungry well past the next coffee break. Then you can thank a Brazil for keeping you from a Danish.

See Recycling Note #8

BREAKFAST IN A SINGLE BITE (*the megavitamin muffin*)

2 eggs, separated	¼ cup soy lecithin
¼ cup unrefined oil	granules

½ cup household honey, or ¼ cup date sugar plus ¼ cup any other natural nonsolid sweetener

½ cup yogurt

½ cup milk or fortified water

1 cup of any of the following or a combination of several: rice polish, bran flakes, peanut meal, wheat germ, gluten flour, natural corn meal, millet meal, whole wheat flour, triticale flour, rye flour, buckwheat flour, soy flour, barley or other bean flour *

¼ cup raw nuts or seeds, coarsely chopped

1 tbsp. protein powder or gland protein powder (optional)

2 tbsp. (or more) malted milk powder, skim milk powder or whey powder

1 tsp. kelp, dulse or sea salt

¼ cup grated fresh apple or dried currants (optional)

¼ cup oats or rye or soybeans or whole wheat or corn or pinto beans in flaked form

¼ cup or less unrefined popped corn (ground), popped millet or puffed wheat

1 tsp. vanilla extract

½ tsp. spice—allspice, nutmeg, cinnamon or pumpkin pie spice

Preheat oven to 375°. Combine first six ingredients in a blender, reserving the egg whites. Beat egg whites until almost stiff and fold into blender mixture. Place remaining ingredients in a bowl and fold in blender mixture. Spoon into bite-sized muffin tins and bake about 15 minutes (watch carefully).

* For better texture, use one part whole wheat, triticale or gluten flour to one part any other flour.

What's Good About It??

Smorgasbordic sounding, isn't it? But all to the good of your digestion, which is aided by the lactose or milk powders; your cholesterol, which is kept in check by the lecithin, the soy, and the pectin (in the apple); your tissue repair, which is kept in progress by the high protein in the gluten, the yeast, peanut meal and protein powders; your mineral supply, which is recharged by the kelp, the yeast and the sprouts.

If you haven't had a bite in days, refuel with one (or two) of these.

✓ CHEMICAL-FREE CHRISTMAS TART

Crust:

1½ cups whole wheat flour
½ tsp. sea salt
pinch allspice and nutmeg

⅓ cup cold-pressed salad oil (virgin olive oil makes the finest crust of all)
4 tbsp. ice cold water

Filling:

½ to 1 cup cranberries
½ orange, pitted and skinned
¼ cup sorghum
2 tbsp. Sweet Something (page 19) or 4 tbsp. date sugar
½ tsp. each powdered cinnamon, nutmeg

and orris root (optional)
2 cups sliced apples, with skins on (if organically raised)
2 tbsp. arrowroot powder
4 tbsp. raw wheat germ

For crust: Mix first four ingredients with a fork until crumbly, then sprinkle in water and combine well. It should be wet enough to be pressed into a pan but not so sticky it adheres to your fingers—soggy graham-cracker consistency.

Put into middle of a lightly oiled pie pan and press into pie shape, crimping edges. Set in refrigerator and proceed with filling.

For filling: Grind cranberries and orange in food mill or chop by hand. Combine with arrowroot and both sweeteners and spices. (Preheat sorghum jar by placing it in pan of hot water to facilitate handling.) Put a layer of apples in pie shell and spread with syrup-cranberry mix. Repeat until fruit is used up. Sprinkle top with wheat germ and a few dots of butter. Bake 10 minutes at 400°. Lower oven to 375° and bake an additional 30 minutes until apples are tender. (The syrup will thicken as the pie cooks.)

Serve warm or cooled with Mistletoe tea.*

See Sources

STEAMED SWEET BUNS

2 cups warm water or fortified water	1 cup soy flour
2 tbsp. bakers' yeast	½ cup wheat germ
3½ cups gluten flour	1 tbsp. homemade sugar

Put warm water into warm bowl. Add yeast and stir until dissolved. Add blended dry ingredients. Beat until smooth. Turn dough out onto floured board and knead thoroughly until dough is smooth and elastic. Shape into buns about the size of your palm but no larger. Cover with towel and let rise about 1 hour.

Carefully poke a cavity into the center of each one (as though you were making belly-buttons), taking care not to go clear through. Put a small dab of soybean jam (see recipe, page 150), some favored relish or a spot of fruit butter. Cover buns again and let rise 20 minutes.

Meanwhile, start a large kettle boiling and insert collapsible steamer. Rub steamer with oil and put in buns with edges touching. Clap on kettle lid and set timer for 20 minutes. Do not peek before then. Test for doneness with cake tester and remove with utmost care after they have cooled slightly. Serve warm with the following sauce.

DUCK SAUCE *(either a sauce or a sweetener for other things)*

2 cups fresh plums, skinned, stoned and mashed

2 cups dried peaches or apricots

1 cup apples or pears, fresh or dried

½ cup cider vinegar

½ cup date sugar

½ cup honey

½ cup pimientos (optional)

Put first three ingredients through food chopper and combine in a deep pot with remaining ingredients. Bring to a boil; lower heat and let simmer for 1 hour.

Preserve in an airtight jar. Flavor is vastly improved if stored for several weeks. Before using, add a little water and honey to taste.

See Recycling Note #3

BLANDINGS *(all sweeteners are in absentia in this beneficial cookie for babies and strict sweet-restricted diets)*

½ cup baby's flour
(see page 31)

4 tbsp. carob powder

2 tbsp. arrowroot
powder

½ cup mild cold-
pressed oil (saf-
flower, the best bet)

1 cup cold fortified
water

½ tsp. salt

4 eggs

Note: All ingredients except water should be at room temperature.

Preheat oven to 400°. Stir flour, carob and arrowroot together. Bring oil, water and salt to a boil over medium heat, lower heat and remove pot from burner. Beat in flour mixture all at once, returning pot to heat and continuing to beat until mixture is smooth and glossy and forms a ball. Transfer to mixing bowl and cool slightly. Add eggs one at a time, beating well with electric mixer after each addition. Continue beating until batter is smooth; then drop by spoonfuls on ungreased cookie sheet.

Bake about 30 minutes or until cookies are puffy and browned. Remove and cool on wire rack.

Those not on sweetener-restricted diets might like to smear some honey on their portions when baby isn't looking.

What's Good About It??

A baby's flour like barley and a thickener like arrowroot are "pabulumatic," that is, digested easily and beneficially by all (which is more than you

can say quite often about wheat and cornstarch).
Barley also contains lots of calcium and more protein
per ounce than buckwheat, cornmeal or whole wheat.
Should you like to add even more protein to this
already admirable cookie, replace the carob with
food yeast. (You can meet 5 percent of your daily
protein allowance by adding only two tablespoons
to your daily fare. Fair enough?)

ECOLOGICAL ECLAIRS *(self-frosting, too!)*

2 tbsp. cornstarch or
tapioca flour
½ cup minus 4 tbsp.
whole wheat or rye
flour
½ cup cold-pressed
oil (room tempera-
ture)

1 cup cold water
½ tsp. salt
4 eggs (room temper-
ature)
4 tbsp. carob powder
¼ tsp. rum extract
(optional)
¼ tsp. nutmeg

Preheat oven to 400°. Mix cornstarch with flour.
Combine oil, water and salt in a saucepan. Bring
to a boil over medium heat. Remove from burner
and turn heat to low. Add flour mixture all at once,
beating constantly to combine smoothly. Return pot
to heat and continue beating until mixture is smooth
and forms a ball (a minute or two). Add nutmeg
extract.

Transfer mixture to a mixing bowl and cool
slightly. Add eggs one at a time, beating well after
each addition (for best results do this with electric
mixer). Continue beating until mixture is smooth
and glossy.

Divide dough into two equal portions in two
bowls. Spread 1 tablespoon of the first batter in
wells of madeline or eclair pan (lacking either of

these, try a cornstick pan). Mix sifted carob powder into second batter and put 1 tablespoon of that mixture atop the first in the pan, smoothing with a dull knife. (You may mix carob into all the batter and make an entire batch of very dark eclairs, as an alternative.)

Bake in the lower part of the oven for 30 minutes or until browned and puffy. Turn oven off and let eclairs sit within an extra 10 minutes. Remove and cool on a wire rack.

The carob batter will give pastries a self-frosted look. To stuff and serve, cut tops off carefully with a very sharp knife, pluck out any soft dough inside and fill with Sweet Something (page 19) or any cream filling you especially flavor. Replace lids.

INKSPOTS *(a company cookie . . . boiled in molasses)*

2 cups whole wheat flour, sifted (if you're in a non-pecuniary mood, substitute ¼ cup ground poppy seeds for the flour)	4 eggs, slightly beaten
	2 tbsp. oil
	1 cup all-purpose honey
1 tbsp. date sugar	1 cup mixed molasses (see Stocking Up)
	¼ pound poppy seeds

Mix together flour, sugar, eggs, oil. Knead until smooth (about 5 minutes). Roll out to ¼-inch thickness on floured board, then cut into 2-inch squares. Fold over into triangles and prick tops with fork.

Bake on greased cookie sheet at 350° for about 15 minutes.

Bring honey-molasses mix to a boil, stirring constantly. Drop cookies into this; after 3 minutes, add poppy seeds. Stir without letup until cookies are a rich brown. Sprinkle with 2 tbsp. cold water, stir well and remove from heat. Place on a greased platter. Separate cookies with wet hands. Chill.

Store between layers of wax paper. Eat before the week's up. Makes about four dozen.

UNBIRTHDAY CAKE *(a sensuous second cousin of gingerbread, less spicy and therefore more all-occasion—made in the blender, no bowls needed)*

3 eggs	*¾ cup soybean flour*
½ cup unsulphured molasses	*¼ cup brewer's yeast*
	¾ cup oil
¼ cup blackstrap molasses	*1 tbsp. baking powder (aluminum-free)*
1 tsp. ginger	*½ raw apple, finely shredded*
1 tsp. allspice	
1 tsp. cinnamon	

Put all ingredients except apple in blender, in order listed. The oil thickens with the eggs so add it after the flour. The baking powder makes the dough rise, so add that last. Preheat oven to 325–350°.

Pour into a properly oiled loaf pan, casserole, large cake pan, whatever (*you,* and you alone, know what sort of shaped cake you relish. They don't all have to look like cartwheels). Sprinkle top with apple.

Bake at 325° or 350° until done (about an hour). Longer, lower-temperature baking prevents bottom from browning prematurely and is productive of a better flavor overall.

This should give you about 24 servings, each of which will contain only 150 calories.

What's Good About It??

You can feel justifiably virtuous about feeding these crumbs to the birds or the fowl or the four-footed strays, or whatever is lurking out there beyond your porch or windowsill. Besides the staunchly nutritious blackstrap molasses (a sort of be-all, it is 50 percent natural sugar and contains the entire B-vitamin complex), brewer's yeast will supply you with one of the few chances you have of getting selenium into your system. And selenium, we are told, is a powerful protector against the effects of mercury pollution. Selenium can't be artificially duplicated. So don't make the yeast an optional ingredient here.

Also note that considerable protein is supplied by the soy flour which has little gluten (and therefore little starch and therefore little to contribute to the widening of the waistline) but is 40 percent protein, and a good calcium source as well.

FAT CHANCES Foods to Fatten or Unfatten

COCOA PUFFS

4 egg whites
2 tbsp. lecithin granules
4 tbsp. date sugar or fruit sugar
2 tbsp. carob powder

1 tbsp. food yeast or protein powder (optional)
dash vanilla extract (optional)

Begin beating egg whites and gradually add rest of ingredients. Continue to beat until very stiff but not dry. Drop by teaspoonfuls on wax paper-covered cookie sheet.

Bake at 275° for an hour or until set. Leave out until puffs are cool and crisp, then store (they store beautifully) in a tight container.

Calories: 10 each (24 puffs).

What's Good About It??

Carob has a 2 percent fat content (compared to the horrifying 52 percent registered by chocolate). It is kind to the liver, unlike cocoa, and doesn't leach the body of B vitamins during digestion, as refined sugar does. (When it comes to whomping up business for bicarb, nothing beats sugar!) Lecithin is a wonder worker, most noted for its ability to lower blood cholesterol. Renowned as a natural preservative, too, it will make these puffs last and last. Make lots and lots.

SEVEN UPPER *(seven sprouted grains in this super-juice)*

Seven kinds of sprouted* seeds, preferably:

sunflower	*rye*
sesame	*oats*
millet	*alfalfa*
lentil	

Enough to fill 2 cups (don't let the snappier, peppery ones like lentil and sunflower prevail).

Blend with 1 cup papaya concentrate (or orange juice concentrate) and 1 cup of sprouted soaking water (never toss this out—squirrel it away if you can't immediately use it; it's rich in vitamins and minerals) until everything is nicely amalgamated.

For a real sweetheart of a drink you might add some honey.

What's Good About It??

Germinated seeds are an excellent source of vitamins A, B complex, C, D, G, K, even U, and such

* See Source #9

minerals as calcium, magnesium, phosphorus, chlorine, potassium and sodium. What's more, the vitamin content of something sprouted skyrockets: oats for instance, after five days of germinating, have 500 percent more B_6, 600 percent more folic acid, 10 percent more B_1, and 1,350 percent more B_2, than before sprouting.

Incidentally, you may steam the sprouts before juicing. (Steamed rye tastes just like wild rice to some people.) Be sure to include your children in this food-without-farming experiment.

See Recycling Note #15

PROTEIN WAFERS *(makes seventy-five weight-watching wafers: true economy-gastronomy in action)*

½ *cup carob powder*	*1 tbsp. any natural*
½ *cup high protein*	*sweetener*
flour (see page 30)	*3 tbsp. oil*
½ *tsp. salt*	¼ *cup water*
	chia nuts

Sift the flour with carob and salt. Blend oil, sweetener and cold water. Pour over flour and mix into soft ball. Knead a few minutes. Roll out very thin on a board (or between layers of wax paper) peppered with chia seeds. Mark off with a dull knife into 1-inch squares. Bake in a moderate 325° oven until golden brown.

What's Good About It??

A craving for chocolate, say some medical researchers, may actually be a craving for vitamin E, chocolate being one of the few things in our diet which contain large amounts of E. After making sure your E intake is adequate, satisfy your cravings with carob, an ingredient of low visibility in too many culinary undertakings. A calorically prudent food, too.

MUGUBGUB *(a mung bean sweet for calorie counters)*

1⅓ cups rinsed mung beans

3 cups plain or fortified water

½ tsp. salt or potassium chloride

1 cup apple juice concentrate

2 envelopes unflavored gelatin

½ cup household honey

Combine beans, water, and salt or potassium chloride. Bring to a boil over moderate heat, cover tightly and simmer until very tender (about 35 minutes), stirring now and again. Drain, if necessary, and combine beans with ½ cup of apple juice concentrate; puree in blender. Set aside.

In a small saucepan, sprinkle gelatin over remaining juice, put over low heat and stir constantly until heated and completely dissolved. Remove from heat, add honey. Combine gelatin mixture and bean mixture thoroughly. Turn into ungreased 8-inch square pan.

Chill until firm. Cut into squares just before serving and if desired roll them in homemade sugar. Refrigerate without the sugar coating, however.

Makes about 36 squares.

What's Good About It??

Mung's the word if you're interested in a vegesweet, because it's low in calories (thirty to a half cup) and high in vitamins C and A, with respectable amounts of calcium and phosphorus.

SNUFKINS *(plain, fruitless, toaster bread, nonfattening)*

½ cup fortified water
1 tbsp. bakers' yeast
2 tbsp. honey
4 tbsp. salad oil
2 tbsp. Tiger's milk or vanilla-flavored protein powder (optional)

1 cup whole wheat flour
½ cup oat flour (grind some rolled oats in your blender)
2 tbsp. food yeast (optional)
½ tsp. cinnamon

Preheat oven to 400°. Dissolve yeast in water and let bubble 5 minutes. Add honey, half the oil, food yeast, Tiger's milk powder and flours. Knead briefly on floured board and roll into an informal rectangle. Arrange in a greased rectangular pan and puncture with tines of kitchen fork or nubs of kitchen knife. Sprinkle with cinnamon and dribble with remaining 2 tbsp. oil.

Bake at 400° for 15 to 20 minutes (*not* till brown). Cut into squares, fold each one in foil and refrigerate.

When ready to eat, unwrap, pop into a wide-slice toaster and toast lightly and quickly till browned.

GREMLINS *(fancy, fruity, unfatty)*

Follow directions above, making these changes: Replace oat flour with ½ cup dry Muesli. Add ½ tsp. almond extract and pinch of mace. Sprinkle top of dough with poppy seeds and currants. You may also (for a chocolaty Gremlin) replace part of flour with carob powder.

PUDGE *(fudge for fat people)*

2 tbsp. cornstarch	1 tbsp. pure vanilla
2 cups fortified water	¼ tsp. almond extract
½ cup household honey	3 tbsp. gelatin
	3 tbsp. carob powder

Mix cornstarch with ¼ cup of fortified water. Bring ¾ cup of the water to a boil. Combine the two (it should thicken immediately) and add the next three ingredients. Set entire mixture in freezer until it is partly frozen. Set aside while you beat remaining cup of water with gelatin and carob in blender until fluffy (and until gelatin is dissolved). Add cold mixture to blender by spoonfuls and let it whip up. If it gets too thick, add a bit of cold water. Pour mixture into glass baking dish and refrigerate. Let set until very cold.

If desired, cut into cubes or squares and roll in additional carob powder mixed with arrowroot powder and allow to dry at room temperature. (They take on additional sweetness as they dry.)

Very skinnyfying stuff.

SLUDGE *(fudge for skinny people)*

½ cup sifted carob powder	⅓ cup maple syrup
½ cup malted milk powder	¼ cup peanut butter
¼ cup soy oil	2 tbsp. hot water
	½ cup chopped nuts
	1 tsp. pure vanilla

Combine first two ingredients. Add oil and syrup.

Stir in everything else and combine well. Chill well after packing in a suitably greased refrigerator dish.

SUGAR-FREE STRUFOLI *(add some cachet to your cookie cannister)*

> 2½ *cups whole wheat pastry flour*
> 4 *eggs plus 1 yolk*
> ¼ *cup soy margarine*
> *dash salt*
> ½ *tsp. lemon peel, grated (unsprayed)*
>
> 2 *cups oil for deep cooking*
> 1½ *cups blended honey*
> 1 *tsp. orange peel, grated (unsprayed)*

Place flour on board, making a well in center. Put eggs, yolk, softened margarine, salt and lemon peel in well. Mix thoroughly, working dough with hands as in the making of noodles. Shape into very small balls the size of marbles and fry in hot oil, a few at a time, until golden brown.

Heat honey gently (grease the saucepan before putting honey in to facilitate cleaning later) and add orange peel. As soon as balls are fried, run them briefly over absorbent toweling and drop into honey. Take them up with a strainer and place on serving dish, piling them into conical mounds. Cool.

What's Good About It??

Not thinnifying this. But honey is a good carbohydrate. And its goodness is greatness when it is unfiltered and raw. Raw honey contains glucose oxidase, an enzyme added to honey by the bees, which releases hydrogen peroxide which in turn destroys bacteria. Honey will not ferment as long as it contains no more than 19 percent water.

In ancient times it was a courtesy of the Romans to welcome respected guests with some honey, fresh from the hives. Why not welcome yours with some honey-rich Strufoli fresh from the oven?

See Recycling Note #16

APPLES WHEY (*more super-manna . . . in a non-solid state*)

½ cup apple juice
1–2 tbsp. apple (or other) blossom honey
½ cup yogurt plus 2 tbsp. whey powder
1–2 tbsp. brewer's yeast powder

1 egg (separated for the nonhurry-up version)
2 tbsp. toasted wheat germ
2 ice cubes
apple ice cubes, optional

For a one-foot-out-the-door breakfast, put everything but ice cubes in blender. Liquify and feed in ice cubes one at a time. Liquify and serve in a glass clink-full of apple juice cubes.

Nonhurry-up version: Beat egg white until stiff. Fold this into the blender-beaten ingredients. Either way, enough for one.

What's Good About It??

Why yogurt instead of milk here? Because yogurt is milk in a super-digestible form. More than 90 percent of it is digested within an hour. And incidentally, honey is richer in mineral salts than either mother's or cow's milk, so you are reaping the benefits of both here. As for the egg (can anything bad be said about it?), between the white (10 percent protein) and the yolk (16 percent protein) it has a better distribution of amino acids (the basic components of protein) than any other food. Put that in your mug and drink it.

See Recycling Note #10

Sugaring Off—an intermission

read on

• Hack Stuff: Simmer ¼ tsp. anise seed and ¼ tsp. thyme in 2 cups water for 15 minutes. Stir in 1 cup household honey. Sip as needed for persistent cough.

• Moscow with the Mostest: The Soviet Union is the world's single largest producer of sugar—about 9 million tons a year compared to Cuba's 4 million and the United States' 6.4 million.

• Fast Fat: Adding just ¼ cup of plain sugar to your daily diet will result in a weight gain of twenty-four pounds at year's end.

• Self-Sweetening Cereal: Instead of honey or molasses, cook your morning's porridge with the addition of diced dried fruits, or just grate a fresh apple into the simmering pot.

• Sugar & the Male Hormone: Tests conducted at the Guy's Hospital Medical School in London revealed that plasma testosterone levels fell by an average of 34.3 percent in subjects fed oral glucose (sugar). Hormone levels did not return to normal until two and a half hours later.

• Pepsi Degeneration? More than any other single food item, according to nutritionists, soft drinks pose the greatest threat to blood sugar levels. Yet in 1973, the average American *increased* his annual soft drink consumption by 1.6 gallons (to 31.9), accounting for a total of 4.46 billion cases of soda pop sold, hypoglycemia notwithstanding. (According to *Beverage Industry Magazine*.)

To be continued . . .

REMEDIES Sweetstuff in Sickness and in Health

√ **GINSENG FIZZ** *(an uncommon iced tea)*

1 tbsp. powdered or minced ginseng root	about 4 tbsp. heather honey
1 tbsp. whole cloves	2 cups sparkling water or club soda
1 cinnamon stick	some ice cubes
2 cups boiling water	
shredded orange peel and orange quarters	

Steep ginseng root and spices and peel and honey in boiling water for 15 minutes. Strain and put into an ice-cube-filled pitcher with orange quarters. Pour in sparkling water and serve, adding more honey as desired.

What's Good About It??

A by-the-by byproduct of this superplant (the Asiatic varieties are favored over their domestic counterparts) is that it relieves fatigue by strengthening the endocrine glands and stimulating the whole body. (The Russians call it an "adaptogen.")

So it would seem that heather honey is in fealty with good old (4000 years or more) ginseng, since *its* curative properties, according to the Scots, are equally remarkable. Heather honey is murky and thickish with lots of tiny air bubbles that give it a characteristic sparkle. You may not like it, but it has two qualities that may ingratiate it to you: a high mineral content and an unforgettable aroma.

As for Siberian superroot? Take the tea and see.

Note: To make Bathtub Ginseng: Quadruple quantities four times.

UPSY-DAISY *(an uplifting cream for face and chin)*

Take some of yesterweek's yogurt (one face-worth), and add 1 tbsp. honey and 2 tbsp. soaked and drained (save the water for tea) dandelion leaves (or roots or any part of the flower). Apply this mask to the face and chin and neck for at least 20 minutes (preferably during a long nap or overnight).

What's Good About It??

The dandelion is a member of the daisy family and is rich in vitamin A, so essential for healthy skin. Yogurt's good effects are easily explained by its rich protein, calcium and acid content. Acts as a milk bleach, too.

A BOTANICAL TOOTHPOWDER

Combine 2 tbsp. dried raspberry leaves with ¼ cup baking powder (and a minute drop of oil of natural raspberry-flavored extract).

What's Good About It??

Raspberry leaves are a time-honored tartar-taker-offer. The tea made from these leaves (rich in iron and vitamin C) is also considered beneficial in strengthening gum tissue.

A teeth twofer.

MOSS SAUCE FOR A SORE THROAT *(yours or a younger one)*

Soak and drain ½ cup of Irish moss * in water for 10 minutes. When drained, add to 6 cups of water along with thinly-pared and sliced rind of 1 lemon (should be organic and well washed) plus the juice of that lemon and a pinch of salt. Boil for 10 minutes, then simmer for 10. Strain and sweeten with a mild honey (such as grapefruit, tupelo, or willow herb, if available).

What's Good About It??

Irish Moss (or carrageen), which is 55 percent gelatinous material and 10–15 percent mineral salts, is a remarkable edible marine plant that contains the minerals our bodies need in near-perfect balance (a better bet, in other words, than Jell-O). And after your sore throat is a thing of the past, you can make pie crusts, jellies, drinks, even mousses (see page 61) with the rest of the package that will boost your health considerably.

* *See Source #10*

CONDIMENT #1: A COUGH SYRUP

To equal parts of dandelion honey and lemon water (lemon juice watered down), add a quarter-part soy lecithin granules. Heat gently and spoon out as needed.

What's Good About It??

Dandelion honey is a time-honored specific against respiratory gripes and is especially beneficial in cases of bronchial ills, it's said. Likewise, lecithin strengthens nerve tissue and should be taken regularly during any spell of the down-and-outs.

CONDIMENT #2: A SLEEPING SYRUP

The bear is not the only one who dreams of honey (as the proverb goes). You will too when you take some of this And-So-To-Sleep-Stuff: One glass of goat's milk (the most digestible and nutritious of all milks, it is closest to mother's milk and contains more vitamins, minerals, fats and proteins than any other milk), blended with 2 or more tbsp. ripe honey, a twist of lemon, and some whey powder (optional). Heat gently, drink gently and sleep gently.

ARF-AND-ARF *(rich cream yogurt, a sumptuous specific for anything that ails your infirm best friend)*

Scald 1 pint of half-and-half and, when it has cooled, stir an additional pint of half-and-half into it. Add 1 tbsp. plain yogurt and 3 tbsp. whole milk powder. Stir well or mix by electric blender. Pour into cups and prepare according to your usual method of yogurt-making.

Serve with crushed sweet biscuit atop, a bit of honey, or however your hound's sweet tooth is best assuaged.

ARF-AND-ARF-PLUS *(for people with very sensuous tastes)*

Begin with 1 quart of real whole raw (if you can find it) honest to Elsie cow's cream and resist the urge to scald it even though it's customary. Put half the cream into blender with ½ cup of plain *fresh* yogurt. Blend, pour into yogurt cups. Repeat blending of remaining cream with another ½ cup plain yogurt. Pour into yogurt cups.

Proceed according to your usual yogurt-making ritual. Resulting yogurt will be very, very thick and very, very unforgettable.

Sweeten if you must gild the lily.

See Recycling Note #20

CAMOMILE CHARMS *(a sort of herbal lifesaver, if you will)*

6 tbsp. gelatin	2 tbsp. fresh or dried
2 cups hot apple juice,	camomile (second
thinned with an ad-	choice: camomile
ditional ½ cup hot	teabags)
water (organic, if	1 tsp. anise flavoring
you really care)	

Steep camomile in apple juice and discard leaves. Put juice in blender and gradually add gelatin (making sure juice is still quite warm). Blend till foamy and add anise to take foam back. Strain through a cloth.

Let set until all foam has risen to top, skim off, and pour into a square freezer container. Refrigerate until good and stiff.

Run hot water over bottom until entire candy block is dislodged. Cut into 16 tiny charm-sized cubes. Spread on cookie sheet and freeze. Later put into freezer container. Defrost for eating.

Calories: 22 each.

What's Good About It??

Camomile (which means "ground apple" and has a scent faintly, pleasantly appley) is a sort of miracle herb. What it doesn't do (it is said to be an antidote for aging, a cure for the riled stomach, and a mild soporific, to name a few of the benefits it bestows) you probably don't need. To boot, it's said that the apple and its juice have a greater ability than any other food to absorb poisons from the digestive tract. And besides, did you know that thanks to its pectin, the apple is a superior aid to the digestion of protein? 'Tis.

SUPERBOWLS Sugar-free Cereals and Snacks

FROSTY FLAKES *(in the granola genre but nutless)*

3 cups oat flakes
(or rolled oats)
1 cup millet flakes
1 cup buckwheat
flakes
1 cup soy flakes or
soya granules
1 cup corn or rice
flakes
½ cup toasted peanut
meal (you may sub-
stitute wheat germ)

1 cup millet grits or
meal
¼ cup unrefined vege-
table oil
½ cup light carob
syrup
hot water
oil of orange, a bit (not
a must) or cinna-
mon extract

Combine dry ingredients according to your likes. Add enough hot water to syrup to dissolve. Add flavoring oil. Mix into dry ingredients. Add more water until moist. Add oil.

Spread on cookie sheet and toast at 325° till crisp.

Cereal-making note: For an individually coated, crisper, more frosted product, mix dry sugar (date, homemade sugar, etc.) with wet, rather than dry, ingredients. Adding dry ingredients to wet ones will result in a crunchier, more peanut-brittle-textured cereal.

See Recycling Note #14

What's Good About It??

After this, you'll never go back to factory-made flakes. (Or did you already know that cornflakes are processed first by a lye bath, then cooked in steam, then mixed in a flavoring syrup that's largely sugar, then rolled under seventy-five tons of pressure, then toasted into total lifelessness and then delivered to you enticingly packaged?)

Wholesome, handcrafted and perishable, this is a multigrain cereal with all its E and B vitamins intact. And don't omit the millet if it's new to you. As a Northern Chinese first cousin of corn, it's high in lecithin and calcium. And anyway, how many people on your block are having Chinese cornflakes for breakfast today???

GROATMEAL *(a good not-so-ready-to-eat cereal)*

¾ *cup raw or pre-roasted buckwheat groats*

2 *cups "enriched" water or milk*

buckwheat honey, honey cream or any homemade sugar

a frugal pinch of cardamom

cream

If you're really serious, begin by roasting the raw groats in a suitably heavy skillet over a medium burner or in the oven, browning them lightly and evenly. Meanwhile, bring water or milk to a boil. Stir in groats slowly and stir hard until gruel is smooth. Turn heat off, replace pot top, and go away for 30 minutes or thereabout.

Sprinkle in cardamom, add buckwheat honey or lace with honey cream. Pour on cream or milk.

What's Good About It??

So what if buckwheat isn't *usually* conjugated with cardamom, which is customarily a component of mulled wine. But how many times were you planning to have *that* this week? It's a good combination because cardamom is herbaceous and hardy, too. And did you know that buckwheat is an herb, not a grain, and that it is one of the rare commercially grown crops that is not routinely sprayed with pesticides? True. And like honey that comes from its blossoms, it's rich in phosphorus and potassium.

See Recycling Note #6

TWO THERMO-CEREALS

Outdoor Porridge

The Night Before: Fill a thermos ⅓ full of cracked wheat, cracked millet, or cracked wild rice (if you are celebrating something). Add a pinch of nutmeg, a pinch of salt. Fill remainder of thermos with fortified water. Seal immediately and let flavors marry overnight.

The Morn After: Uncork and stir in a tablespoon or two of Sweet Nothing or any homemade sugar.

Indoor Porridge

The Night Before: Heat a heavy skillet and toast ¾ cup buckwheat flour in it (if you haven't been completely won around to the flavor, temper a bit with ½ cup wheat germ flour) for at least 5 minutes. Spoon into a thermos and cover with 1½ cups boiling sweet stock. Add salt. Mix well and cork up bottle.

The Morn After: To serve, add buckwheat honey to taste or if you've made the soybean jam on page 150, spoon it in, as a savory instead-of.

See Recycling Note #6

BLACKSTRAP BRANOLA *(a cold comfort cereal)*

1 cup dry-roasted rye flour

2 cups plain bran flakes

1 cup dry-roasted coarse bran (organic)

1 cup toasted wheat germ

½ cup raisins, minced

½ cup malted milk powder

½ tsp. salt

¼ cup rice bran oil

¼ cup blackstrap molasses blended with ½ cup buckwheat honey

Preheat oven to 250°. Start, if you can, with whole rye berries and grind them fresh for the best flavor (which surprisingly is much like malted milk, who knows why). Combine with coarse bran.

Toast flours in a heavy skillet over medium heat, stirring all the while. Combine flours in mixing bowl with everything else that's nonliquid, except salt.

Heat molasses and honey, oil and salt in a small pot until mixture is thin. Pour this over cereal, blending carefully to spread evenly. Bake in 250° oven 1 hour (turning every 20 minutes with spatula).

Let cereal cool in bowl where it may form some lumps (that's okay). When cool, break up clumps and put into a tightly closed jar or can. Refrigerate.

Makes about six cups.

What's Good About It??

One caveat about bran aside (if yours wasn't organically raised, it will be fairly thoroughly impregnated with whatever pesticides were used in the fields where it grew; the outer bran layers of the kernel are where the plant stores these residues): there could hardly be a better protein source as grains go (it outranks barley and buckwheat and rye) and it is in addition a supernacular source of that elusive B vitamin, inositol, also present in luxurious amounts (as are the other B vitamins) in blackstrap molasses. The latter also contains large amounts of iron (but if you have no taste for it use all buckwheat honey, which has four times the iron of other honeys).

And here is another noteworthy omission to contemplate: When grains are refined for cereal, the essential mineral zinc is removed, the not-at-all-essential metal cadmium becoming concentrated in its stead. (Cadmium is also found frequently as a contaminant of refined sugar.) Just in case you needed one more reason to boycott cereals not your own.

See Recycling Note #24

STICKY WICKET *(a raw spoon-fed snack)*

4 cups combination
(any proportion you
like): plain puffed
rice, puffed wheat,
puffed corn and/or
popped millet and/
or unseasoned fresh-
ly made popcorn
and/or buckwheat,

rye or rice flakes
(most of the above
available at most
natural food shops)
½ cup household
honey
½ cup soy or dairy
butter

Preheat oven to 300°. Gently heat water and honey with butter in a glass jar in pot of boiling water. Stir this into large bowl where you've pre-mixed the popped and puffed grains, combine well and spread on a greased cookie sheet. Put in oven at 300° to *toast* (do not cook!) till light brown.

Dump back in bowl and eat with spoon.

What's Good About It??

Uncut, unedited, uncooked and not fattening, either. Good because the grains supply sulphur, and a sulphur-poor diet often results in a horrible craving for sugar. Did you ever think preventive medicine could be this much fun??

Sugaring Off—an intermission

read on

• Settling Down: A favorite drink of early settlers was made by boiling down maple sap to three-fourths of its original volume, fermenting with yeast and flavoring with spruce twigs.

• Only Yesterday: "The consumption of sugar and

other relatively pure carbohydrates has become so great during recent years that it presents a serious obstacle to the improved nutrition of the general public. . . ." (Council on Foods and Nutrition, American Medical Association, *1942.*)

• Rather than Raisins . . . keep a blueberry barrel in your pantry. Fresh sun-dried blueberries were often kept at hand in homesteaders' kitchens and used as a substitute for raisins.

• Black Bottoms (The Undoing Of): To guard against burnt bottoms, make outside cookies slightly larger than inside cookies on baking sheet. To flatten any type of cookie, cover a flat-bottomed glass with piece of cheesecloth wrung out in cold water and press cookies to thin.

• The Faster-Faster Affair: Thanks largely to stepped-up sugar consumption, the incidence of dental caries in this country is progressing six times faster than the needed number of dentists can be trained, according to Michael Jacobsen's Center for Science in the Public Interest. (And if you're an average American you have five unfilled cavities.)

• Botanical Cocoa (or White Cocoa, in kid-ese): Combine 1 cup milk with 1 tbsp. milk powder and 1 tsp. slippery elm powder (a powdered tree bark beloved by the American Indians for its stomach soothing properties), 1 tsp. honey and blend. Heat gently in double boiler. Fine baby's beverage.

To be continued . . . .

SHAKING & SPREADING STUFF Jams, Jellies, Fruit Salts and More

JELLY JELLY *(made with agar-agar)*

2 tbsp. agar-agar flakes or 1 tbsp. granules

2½ cups blended honey (a good balance would be orange blossom-white sage-clover)

¾ cup strained lemon juice

lemon verbena leaves (optional)

Dissolve agar-agar in 1 cup of honey and gently heat this for about 10 minutes (longer is better to make certain jelling has taken place). Add remaining honey and lemon juice, and heat through.

Remove from heat, skim and pour into hot sterilized glasses. If you are feeling old-fashioned, a lemon verbena leaf in each glass is a nice accessory. Cover with paraffin (unless you're only making half the recipe for immediate use). Makes five glasses.

What's Good About It??

There are 9,000 taste buds that dot your tongue, throat, pharynx, inside your cheeks and the surface of the upper and lower plates. So why batter them down with humectants, antimycotics, buffering agents, artificial flavors, enhancers, and acidifying agents? (All of these chemicals are crowded into what supermarkets euphemistically pass off as "jelly.") This jelly is the taster's choice, because agar-agar is derived from a Japanese seaweed and therefore contains no animal protein and has a high mineral content. Unlike commercial pectin products which are sour, and must be combined with large amounts of sugar, agar-agar need only be warmed in liquids rather than boiled, thus preserving precious enzymes, minerals and vitamins. An unbeatable *better* breadspread, this. Agreed, agreed?

GRINDER JAM *(a nearly instant marmalade)*

Soak some dried apricots briefly in hot water. Drain. Run through electric or manual food mill, using fine blade. To each cup of fruit add ½ cup comb honey combined with 1 cup orange blossom honey. Blend thoroughly, adding some shreds of dried unsprayed orange or tangerine peel (this is an optional amenity).

Store in sterilized jars at least two weeks. Resultant jam will have the customary marmalade texture.

What's Good About It??

Chemical overcrowding in our foods has become something of an un-Christian science and nowhere is the battle busier than in your jam jar. The chemicals, besides all that sugar, include a good part of the nearly 203,000 pounds of totally artificial color dumped into confectionary-type foods yearly. So jam is certainly not a junior food unless it's made with honey. (Honey, according to researchers, has been shown to have a beneficial influence on the retention of calcium by infants, too.)

To hard-boiled jam-makers, this recipe may seem a bit heretical (No boiling? No straining, no stirring down? No sieving?) but maybe the two weeks of waiting will satisfy the puritanical pangs.

See Recycling Note #21

RICE ICING

4 eggs
3/4 cup oil (rice bran would be appropriate if you're feeling flush)
3/4 cup blended honey

Blend until smooth and thick.

Blend the above and add:

4 tbsp. carob powder
1 cup cooked brown rice

Variation: For Red Rice Frosting, add beet juice (and/or enough paprika powder to produce desired tint) to liquid in which rice is cooked.

What's Good About It??

Brown rice is rum stuff (but watch out for the ordinary hulled varieties which, besides being denuded of nutrients, are heavily sprayed and fumigated during their lives in the fields). Reputedly, there are 7,000 different types of rice but whichever one you have is, if it's whole, a good source of vitamin E and an excellent source of niacin. Like oats, rice contains all the essential amino acids, but it is low in protein, so use this on top of a high-protein cake (or, conversely, if you have a low-protein cake, see the formulas for high-protein frosting elsewhere in this book).

TWO TOAST FROSTINGS

Did you know that bread is sweeter when it's toasted? Dextrinization is at work. Destruction of B_1 is also at work, but let's ignore that while we have our jam pots poised.

• Indoor jam: Put dried apricots and one packet of Mu tea leaves for each cup of fruit into hot water. Drain and run through food grinder (fine blade). Add 1½ cups liquid or solid honey to each cup of herbed fruit. Blend thoroughly. Store in sterilized jars.

• Outdoor jam: Boil 8 ounces date sugar with 8 ounces maple sugar or maple syrup. Boil till it threads and put in 1 pound of fresh picked-over berries. Bring to a second boil. Pour on platter and set in sun for 3 days. Turn into jelly jars.

TWO ICE CREAM SAUCES

Fake Fudge Sauce

¼ *cup carob powder*
⅓ *cup date sugar*
⅔ *cup soy milk, nut milk or milk milk*
pinch salt

2 *tbsp. dry malt (optional)*
2 *tbsp. oil or butter*
½ *tsp. vanilla*

Mix carob and sugar. Add milk, malt and salt. Bring to a boil and simmer with oil, stirring the while (about 5 minutes). Add flavoring. Store in refrigerator.

Honey Dripper

½ cup butter
1 cup household honey

1 quart fruit juice (not too tart)

Melt butter in double boiler. Whip honey energetically. Heat mixture until honey dissolves completely; then add juice. Continue to heat until syrup is desired consistency.

Makes about one pint.

DOUGHNUT GLAZE

2 tbsp. melted home-made butter or co-conut oil
2 tbsp. thick honey (pine, heather, buck-wheat or other)

1 tbsp. carob powder
¼ tsp. vanilla or maple flavoring

Melt butter over low heat. Stir in carob, honey and flavoring. Dip doughnuts in glaze and set in refrigerator to harden.

For a lighter glaze: omit carob and add soy milk powder, ground coconut or rice polish.

SUGARLESS GLAZED FRUIT

1 cup household honey

½ cup water or for-tified water

Bring honey and water to boil in saucepan. Immerse prepared fruit (cherries, whole apples, citrus peels, pineapple chunks or slices, etc.) in this syrup and cook until tender, turning now and then. Remove and drain.

HI-PROTEIN FROSTING *(the fast way)*

> 1 egg white
> dash salt
> ¼ cup mixed molasses
>   *(see Stocking Up)*
>
> ¼ cup toasted sesame
>   seeds

Beat egg white with salt until stiff enough to hold peaks (but not dry). Pour molasses in a fine stream over egg white, beating constantly until frosting holds its shape, about 2½ minutes with electric beater. Fold in sesame seeds. Covers two 8-inch layer cakes.

The slow way:

> ⅔ cup honey
> ⅓ cup fresh coconut
>   milk
> ¼ cup water or for-
>   tified water
>
> ⅔ cup carob powder
> 6 egg whites
> 1 tsp. baking powder
>   (aluminum-free)
> toasted coconut

Combine all ingredients except egg whites, baking powder and coconut. Bring to boil. Turn down heat and simmer. Whip egg whites until stiff. Add baking powder and continue beating until high and creamy. Pour boiling mixture over whites, beating hard. Fold in some coconut, frost cake and sprinkle remaining coconut on top.

SUGAR-FREE MUSTARD *(best made in the winter)*

Cook one box (about 2 ounces) of yellow mustard seed (assuming you're making plain old pantry mustard) in 1 cup of a spiced (tarragon? dill?) vinegar and 1 cup of a spicy honey such as white sage. Simmer until mustard seeds are soft and plumped. Blend well in electric blender and bottle up.

Note: A more exotic but no more expensive mustard may be made from black Indian mustard seeds. Interested?

See Source #1

SUGAR-FREE CATSUP *(best made in the summer)*

2 pounds fresh toma-
toes, cooked and
drained

¼ cup apple cider
vinegar

¾ cup apple blossom
(or other fruit blos-
som) honey

2 tbsp. chopped fresh
dill (or crushed dill
seed)

2 tbsp. fresh chive or
basil

1 tbsp. fresh onion
juice or grated raw
onion

2 tbsp. powdered kelp
or herb salt

1 tsp. celery seed

Combine all ingredients and put half the mixture in blender. Process and decant. Blend the remaining half, combine both mixtures and correct seasoning. Bottle up. Refrigerate. Will keep nicely for a month, maybe more.

VEGETARIAN'S BUTTER #1 *(cowless, sugarless, scrumptious)*

5 pounds onions
(you may replace 1
pound of ordinary
yellow onions with

1 pound of scallions
and leeks)

water

salt

Peel the onions and quarter them. Put the big chunks into a big heavy pot and scantily cover with water (onions contain a lot of liquid). Bring contents to a boil, top with lid and simmer for a full 24 hours (you might place an asbestos pad between the pot and its burner to insure against burning). Check how onions are coming at intervals and add a bit more water (just a bit) if necessary.

Butter is done when it has turned dark brown, and resembles a sort of lumpy honey. Break it up into a paste of uniform consistency, salt to taste and simmer without lid until final excess water evaporates.

Makes about two pints. Delicious on vegetables, pancakes, breakfast breads.

What's Good About It??

Impropaganda on behalf of the onion: recent research conducted in the Soviet Union indicates that onions (and note, preambly, that they are an ancient vegetable having been employed medicinally for more than a thousand years) are valuable in the prevention of heart disease and high blood pressure. The onion is rich in calcium and phosphorus, potassium and vitamin A, and it contains strong germ-killing biochemicals. Low in sodium, and low in calories, its juice helps improve kidney function and speeds excretion of urine. Its utilitarianism aside, the onion numbers among its noble cousins the tulip, orchid and asparagus. Considering the bitter facts about cow's butter these days, onion-butterless you should never be. And what better never-bring-a-tear-to-the-eye form to have it in than this?

VEGETARIAN'S BUTTER #2

Using good scrubbed carrots rather than onions, go through the steps of the preceding recipe.

ZABAGLIONE (EGG CUSTARD SAUCE) (*a zesty desert sauce . . . sans sucre*)

3 egg yolks	½ cup plus 1 tsp.
3 tbsp. household	Marsala or Madeira
honey	wine or a sweetish
	sherry

Put yolks in a bowl and beat until they are light in color; gradually add honey and continue to beat. Add wine and mix thoroughly. Pour into saucepan and cook over high heat. Beat constantly to prevent mixture from boiling or thickening. Remove from heat as soon as it begins to rise and pour into glasses. Chill.

Serves four.

See Recycling Note #10

XOCOALO (*a Mexican chocolate sauce*)

¼ cup pure olive oil	¼ cup peanuts
2 ounces carob pow-	½ tsp. cinnamon
der	1 cup milk
2 tbsp. sesame seeds	1 cup fortified water
½ tsp. anise seeds	¼ cup honey
½ cup almonds	

Heat oil and mix with carob (this procedure nullifies any raw taste that carob sometimes imparts) and set aside. Grind next four ingredients, blend with cinnamon and add to oil and carob. Heat gently, stirring, for 5 minutes, while on the other hand and on the other burner warming the milk and water. Combine these two (using a wire wisk) and add honey. Heat until thickened.

Serve warm or cold. Makes stunning stuff out of stale cake.

FRUIT WURST *(a bioflavinoid butter)*

Soak 5 chopped dates in 3 cups hot water till soft. Drain and blend until smooth with 2 tsp. unsprayed orange or lemon or grapefruit rind, using the bioflavinoid-rich inner (white part) rind.

BREAKFAST SUGAR *(a bioflavinoid flavoring)*

Grind ¼ cup unreconstituted Muesli-style cereal with 1 tbsp. oven- or sun-dried citrus peel (lemon, grapefruit, tangerine, kumquat, orange, lime) in seed mill or blender. When everything is powdery fine, bottle it up in small shaker and store with your spices.

FRUIT STEW *spread*

Soak a mixture (unless you are monogamous in fructose affairs, then substitute your favorite variety) of chopped dried fruit in boiling milk, whey or herb tea to cover. Put in refrigerator for an hour. Drain and mix a little arrowroot or cornstarch with the pot liquor. Heat gently till thickened and return fruit to pot. Eat with a spoon for breakfast or dessert. Or put in blender, process and use as a spread.

MASH *(a fruity sort of flummery)*

1 pint of fresh fruit, washed, peeled and diced

½ cup date sugar

2 tbsp. arrowroot or 1 tsp. alginate powder

¼ cup fortified water or fruit juice

2 ounces fresh lemon juice

dash of salt

Combine everything in a saucepan and bring to a boil slowly, stirring constantly. Boil for 1 minute. Turn out into custard cups and chill. Serve with or without the following.

POSH *(a flummery frosting)*

1 cup unsweetened coconut meal

1 cup warm water

1 tbsp. honey

dash of pure vanilla extract or homemade vanilla

Blend coconut meal and water until smooth; then blend in honey and vanilla.

DOW DING EXTENDER *(Oriental embellishment for your Big Whopper)*

2½ cups roasted and mashed soybeans

2 cups cooked rice

2 tbsp. homemade sugar

1 tsp. salt

1 tbsp. chopped sweet onion

Mix all ingredients together and form a cake. Dry it in the sun or in a low oven for a long time (see if 12 hours will do the trick). Put into a container and cover; let stand for 1 week. Add boiling water to cover, and then add 1 cup rice wine. Keep in airtight container for 6 months to develop full flavor. One heaping tablespoon will add some sweet mystique to your homemade burgers.

UMEBOSHI BURGER SAUCE

2 crushed salted plums (Umeboshi)

1 cup boiling fortified water (see page 20)

¼ cup Duck Sauce or soybean jam

Boil plums in water for 7 minutes. Cool and reheat with jam or sauce. Spoon over broiled burgers.

ROOT RELISH

½ cup raw celery or/and horseradish root

2 cored apples

2 tbsp. honey

1 cup plain yogurt

some vegetable salt

Grate root and apple. Mix with remaining ingredients and freeze till mushy. Stir and refreeze. Remove from freezer 20 minutes before needed. One scoop atop your chopped sirloin some summer day makes for the radicalization of the hamburger: an iceburger!

FAST, UNFATTENING FROSTINGS

With Arrowroot

1 large fresh egg white

4 tbsp. skimmed honey

4 tbsp. arrowroot or as needed

Blend honey and egg white in a small tall bowl (or a measuring cup and use only one beater) with electric mixer. Beat until frothy; then, a spoonful at a time, add arrowroot and continue beating and adding until smooth and thickened. Hardens with refrigeration.

With Yogurt

½ cup homemade
   yogurt
½ cup   half-and-half
   honey
⅓ cup noninstant
   milk powder

1 tbsp. lime juice
1 tbsp. soy butter (or
   the real stuff if you
   aren't boycotting it)

Beat all ingredients together until smooth. Add more milk powder to thicken.

Makes about a fourth of a cup.

See Recycling Note #7

INCONVENIENCE FOODS Special Sweets, Not-So-Ready to Serve

✓ **PLUM JERKY** (*a fruit leather*)

4 cups fully ripe plums (or any other very nice, very soft fruit in season)

honey (maybe) or Fruit Wurst (page 139)
arrowroot starch
cheesecloth or netting

The first ingredient is sun. Don't start without it. Then, on a large table or big cookie sheets, stretch a goodly amount of plastic wrap and secure well with tape at corners.

Meanwhile, in the kitchen, put 4 cups of plums (skins and all, but depitted of course) into blender and blend until mixture is smooth. Sweeten with honey (this may be unnecessary but taste and see).

Pour in small puddles onto plastic wrap (or you can even butter some old window panes instead if your offspring are into Garage Gastronomy).

Protect from insects by stretching netting or cheese-cloth over top and securing to a board placed at either side. Place table in full sun (if weather turns humid, bring table inside).

After 3 or 4 days of sun-drying you should be able to pull the fruit puree off the sheets in whole pieces. Roll up the fruit leather in the wrap. Or dust with arrowroot and roll and tie with ribbons.

Keeps well in a cool place for a month or so —longer in the refrigerator.

What's Good About It??

Dandy candy especially appealing to children because it's something like eating your high school diploma. So the sobering (to you) fact that it is nutritionally heroic stuff will be wasted on the confectionary consciousness of your children. Plum full of protective pectin, vitamin A, and almost twice as much riboflavin as raisins. (Funnily enough, this B vitamin was once known as vitamin G. Tell your kids that too.)

UNCOOKED FRUIT CAKE (*biblical supermanna, cooked by the sun*)

Mix and feed through a manual or electric food grinder:

1 pound pitted dates (or figs)

1 pound seedless un-sulphured raisins

4 dried bananas

Work in:

8 ounces ground almonds

1 cup (or more—if you were frugal with the figs, don't be prudent with the peanuts) peanut meal, toasted

1 cup oat or rice flakes, lightly toasted

Press dough into a cake ring or fancy mold and let harden for an hour or so. Turn out onto plate and set in the sun to dry.

What's Good About It??

There are good baked goods and there are bad baked goods. Then there are good unbaked goods, of which this is one. Doughty and sedentary stuff but scandalously nutritious because it's raw and because all dried fruits are rich in magnesium (which activates more enzymes in the body than any other mineral). Considerable protein is provided by the peanut meal (rich in B_1, riboflavin and niacin, too) so if this isn't real earth food, earth medicine (no less so for having been baked on your veranda), what is?

Note: It is worth seeking out an organic source for your dried fruit. The mass-produced product is most often force-ripened, detergent-cleaned, dehydrator-dried, sulphured, heated and even slightly rehydrated to stimulate the sun-dried product. Shoddy practices at a fancy price.

SPARKLING LEMONADE (*light natural carbonation*)

> peel and juice of 2 lemons (organic if that's feasible)
> ½ cup honey plus 2 tbsp. barleymalt sweetener, or 1 cup of honey
>
> 7 cups boiling water
> ⅛ tsp. bakers' yeast
> raisins
> chia seeds

Slice lemon peels thinly and place them in a

large container with the sweeteners. Pour on boiling water. Let cool until lukewarm. Stir in yeast and lemon juice. Let sit, loosely covered, for 12 hours. Bottle, adding 3 raisins per bottle. When raisins have floated to top (a day or two), chill.

Serve with a pinch of seeds and cracked ice. A sprig of mint is redundant (chia is a member of the mint family) but nice anyway.

What's Good About It??

If heretofore you've saved the lemonade in the house for children's cocktails, repent and retreat. Lemons are a super source of potassium and the older you are the more you need. The chia seeds are here for another reason: Rich in protein, this dwarf-poppyseedlike food is celebrated for its thirst-quenching properties and has long been prized as an energy and endurance food. It appears as a constituent of lemonade courtesy of the Indians of Mexico.

HEALTH NUTS

garbanzo beans (chick-peas), fresh and raw

household cooking oil, fresh (unused before)

dry malt (or additive-free malted milk powder)

corn germ oil

herb salt

toasted sesame seeds, too, if you have them

Soak beans in water for 48 hours. Add fresh water and salt the last 8 hours. Drain and rub in towel to dry.

Put cooking oil in heavy kettle. Have oil 3–4

inches deep. Heat to 425°. Put dried beans in oil a few at a time and cook about 7 to 10 minutes, until golden brown. Remove and drain on paper toweling.

Put into a bowl, add small amount of corn germ oil and salt, sesame and malt (enough oil to assure that other ingredients adhere); stir up and serve while still warm.

Note: You may alternatively omit corn germ oil and just "sugar" beans with fruit sugar powder, honey powder or the dry malt.

What's Good About It??

The garbanzo beans are good eggs. Also known as chick-peas, they are 20 percent protein and contain good supplies of iron, phosphorus and calcium. Or, known as Pois Chiche (which is even nicer), they will contribute some vitamin A and C to your diet. And by any other name, a sprouted garbanzo is a triply fine depot of these nutrients, so fry some, sprout some.

See Recycling Note #12

CARROT ROOT WINE

5 *pounds carrots, old but scrubbed*

4 *pounds raw or brown sugar (it's okay here since fermentation changes sugar to alcohol and carbonic acid)*

6 *organic oranges, cut up*

1 *pound muscat raisins*

2–3 *pieces bruised ginger root*

1 *ounce dry bakers' yeast*

Chop and boil carrots in 2½ gallons of water

until soft. Squeeze carrot mush through cheesecloth bag or porous cloth and mix with sugar, raisins, oranges and ginger.

Set aside until lukewarm and then add yeast, which has first been dissolved in 1 cup warm water. Cover crock and "let it work" in a warm place for 2 weeks, stirring frequently.

Strain and siphon into sterilized bottles and cork lightly. Lift, then push down corks every day, and, when fermentation has stopped, seal tightly by thrusting corks down forcefully. The wine at this time will have changed from a brick tone to a gingery, blooming orange.

CARROT ROOT VINEGAR

Follow all the above steps but, after corking lightly, allow air to make contact with wine (that is, continue to cork lightly) until your taste buds tell you you have vinegar.

A fine gift for carrot-fond friends.

CANNED CANDY *(parental guidance required)*

The only ingredient is a can of evaporated milk. Submerge can in boiling water for 5 hours. Put into the freezer immediately. Keep there for another 5 hours.

Open can and eat (the innards are now a rich taffylike candy).

Note: Great care must be taken to keep the can covered with water during boiling. Otherwise it explodes.

This recipe is sometimes known as Spilt Milk, and it would be very difficult not to cry over it after 10 hours of unrewarded waiting.

STARTERS

Gluten Starter *(a sweet meat-maker)*

> 2 tbsp. fruit juice con-
> centrate
>
> ¼ cup lukewarm wa-
> ter
> 1 cup gluten flour

Combine concentrate and water and add to flour in small bowl. Combine until soft ball is formed. Knead a few minutes until ball is smooth and not too sticky. Put ball in bowl of cold water to cover. Two hours later, take out and knead again, squeezing out starch, and then putting back into cold-water bath. Keep kneading and squeezing at intervals throughout the day, changing the water each time. The entire process should take 8 to 12 hours (by which time the gluten should produce a nearly clear water when soaked).

Slice the dough mass into "cutlets" and put in a pot with a sweetened broth (fruit juice and water) to cook for about 1 hour (bring to a boil, then lower heat and cover pot). When cooled, dredge cutlets (this is a meat substitute, you know) in beaten egg, then wheat germ and breadcrumbs.

Bake in 300° oven for 20 minutes.

Serve in a sweet-and-sour sauce.

Sweet-and-Sour Starter *(a sweeter sour dough-maker)*

> 1 cup orange juice for-
> tified with 4 tbsp.
> orange juice con-
> centrate (or try a
> cherry-juice, cherry-
>
> concentrate combi-
> nation)
> 1 tbsp. bakers' yeast
> 1 cup any whole grain
> flour

Dissolve yeast in warmed fruit juice and let sit

10 minutes. Slowly add flour and mix well. Place in scalded jar or crock. Let sit at room temperature for several days until bubbly and fermented. Stir well and refrigerate.

Starter is now ready for making bread. Use 1 cup starter in any recipe, but feed your starter by adding back one-half of this mixture: 1 cup starter, 1 cup lukewarm sweet water, 1 cup flour. Use your starter about every 10 days. (It will become increasingly sour.)

SOYBEAN JAM *(beautiful beany spread like nobody's mother used to make—good with lobster and pork)*

6 cups soybeans
water or sweet stock
  to cover
½ cup sorghum

3 tbsp. sesame salt
slices fresh ginger (optional)

Put beans in pot with water to cover, 3 inches over beans. Add remaining ingredients. Bring to boil and then simmer for 2 hours, adding more (boiling) water if necessary.

Preserve in airtight jar 6 months or more to develop flavor.

SOY SAUCE SUGARLESS *(To give good friends. How often do you get a gift that's a year in the making?)*

10 cups soybeans*
½ cup sea salt

6 gallons water
½ cup molasses

Mix all ingredients and cook until boiling.

* Use the beans in the above recipe if you are preparing that too.

Lower heat and simmer 5 hours. (This should still leave about 5 gallons of liquid.) Strain.

Pour into a 5-gallon glass jug. Seal airtight. Keep in a frequently sun-lit spot (a window ledge or roof) for 1 year (or more, if your patience is saintly) and the resultant liquid will be a delectable light soy sauce.

Sugaring Off—the last intermission
read on

• "Much of our present dietary trouble arises from the fact that 200 years ago man learned to isolate sugar."—Dr. John Yudkin

• Good, by Gum! If chew you (or your children) must, make it a naturally-come-by cud. Suggestions: squares of honeycomb, fresh licorice root, mastic gum (the Arabs chew it, cook with it and put it in love potions), cardamom seeds (the Indians and Danes find it indispensable, and reputedly it's **a** good coverup for alcoholic breath).

• Now & Then: The original (1848) recipe for Sally Lunn calls for *no sugar.* "In mixing this cake, *add neither sugar nor spice.* They do not improve but spoil it, it would be found on trial. It is the best of tea cakes if properly made . . ." cautions Miss Leslie (1857). Contemporary (1973) formulas for Sally Lunn use half a cup of sugar.

• Blossom Bowl (a nonedible sweet): Dry for three days in the sun: 1 quart rose petals, 1 pint geranium leaves, 1 pint lavender flowers, 1 pint dry rosemary. Add a little salt, cinnamon, allspice, nutmeg, anise, ginger, cloves, orris root. Combine and cap up in apothecary jar for two months. Unveil for special occasion (birthday? anniversary? christening?). Sweetens any kitchen or parlor.

• Undandy Candy: Forty-five years ago when the National Confectioners Association began keeping records, annual candy consumption was under fifteen pounds per person. Today it is a good bad twenty pounds. "My son, eat honey, for it is good" said Solomon (Proverbs 24:13). "Butter and honey he shall eat until he knows to refuse the evil and choose the good" (Isaiah 7:15).

SHORT ORDER SWEETS
Minute-Made Eats in
Less Than Half an Hour

GRAPE ICE

Wash a bunch of grapes well and put into the freezer for 30 minutes. Remove and serve as is as grape ice.

ENERGY CRUNCH *(for one)*

Blend 2 tbsp. honey with 2 tbsp. nut butter. Add 2–3 tbsp. milk powder and a sparse pinch cayenne. Shape into a square about ½ inch thick. Let set, and then press in lots of cracked crunchy nuts.

"WHEATEA" *(a fine tyke tea)*

Combine 6 ounces of milky tea (half one and half the other) with 1 tsp. raw or toasted wheat germ and 1 tsp. honey. Add half a stick of cinnamon.

Bring to a near-boiling point (if you wash your pot with cold water before using, milk won't scald).

Cool slightly and serve with stick and spoon (to eat the germ that collects at the bottom of the cup).

HONEY DROPS

Heat 1 cup orange blossom honey with ½ cup water. Bring to boil and continue boiling to 240°F. on thermometer. Drop one teaspoon at a time into a pan of firmly packed, finely cracked ice.

You'll get hard flat candies, but with some practice you may achieve round ones. Either way, wrap them in wax paper and store.

BROWN LOAFERS (a whole grain mix to make semi-sweet loafs from)

6 cups brown loaf flour (whole wheat, wheat-rye, triticale, graham or a combination of these)
2 cups soy flour
pinch of salt and kelp
1 tbsp. double acting baking powder

1 cup noninstant powdered milk
2½ cups wheat germ
½ cup homemade sugar or ¼ cup homemade sugar and ¼ cup sugarless protein powder *

Mix everything well and keep in airtight jar or cannister in refrigerator. Use ½ to 3 cups of this mix to replace dry ingredients in semi-sweet bread recipes. You may add spices and additional sweetening to taste. A Basic Brown Loafer (with nuts), for instance, goes like this:

* See Stocking Up

Combine 1 cup coarsely chopped nuts with 3 cups of Brown Loafer mix. Stir in 1 egg, 1 cup plain yogurt, ½ cup unrefined vegetable oil and ¼ cup maple or date sugar. Mix well and pour into greased 1-pound loaf tin. Bake 1 hour at 325°. Turn out on rack and cool.

BIG MACADAMIA BARS *(an unrefined celebration)*

(this is the unrefined part)
  ¼ cup each:
    raisins
    dates
    dried peaches or apricots
    prunes
(this is the celebration part)
  ¼ cup coarsely broken macadamia nuts (or you might consider a "mock mac," the filbert, which is half as costly and quite as tasty)
1 ounce (about) of pineapple juice concentrate
2 tbsp. sifted whey, arrowroot or carob powder
edible rice paper (optional) *

Put fruits through food grinder. Combine with nuts and as much juice as you need (if any) to make a soft but not sticky mass.

Combine well and press into a shallow pan predusted with arrowroot, whey or carob powder.

Or, if you are truly celebrating, pack into a rice-paper-lined baking dish.

Dust top with more powder, cover and refrigerate.

When hardened, cut into bars and encapsule individually in see-through wrap.

See Recycling Note #4

* See Source #2

What's Good About It??

Some authorities say that nuts contain more food value per pound than meat, grain or fruits. Allowing for some hyperbole, nut protein *is* more easily handled by the intestinal machinery than any other kind. And there's not another nut that touches the Mac for protein (35.4 percent). If, however, you are in the glum business of accounting for every carbohydrate, you might consider filberts instead with their relatively modest carbohydrate value of 10 percent.

Cheer up and chew. And remember these for Halloween sacks and hanging Christmas socks.

PRESWEETENED COFFEE BAGS *(an upper—no caffeine)*

Dry roast a cup each of two compatible grains such as rye berries and whole wheat berries (spread on a cookie sheet in the oven at a moderate 300-ish degrees). The former are especially exotic when toasted. Then grind grains in coffee mill, food mill, or a sturdy blender (the result need not be fine); mix with 1 tsp. date sugar or nut sugar, add 1 chopped dried fig, pear or date (if you don't plan to keep this around indefinitely), and parcel up in a large patch of cheesecloth or muslin (triple strength) or piece of panty hose (Danskins aren't just for dancing, you know). Tie with a 6-inch length of clean twine, thread or dental floss, and attach I.D tag.

PRESWEETENED TEA BAGS *(a downer—no caffeine)*

Put 1 tbsp. dried herbal tea leaves together with 1 tsp. date or nut sugar and 1 pinch of dried fruit rind (optional), plus 1 clove and/or a shard of vanilla bean into a patch of muslin or cheesecloth and parcel according to the instructions above.

When-you-care-enough-to-send-the-very-best: Stuff a new teapot full of handmade bags of brew like these, fancy-wrap and ship out to the lucky recipients.

VITAMIN CRUNCH BARS *(a hand-held confection of real value)*

½ cup soy powder (or
   you may toast ½
   cup soy flour)
½ cup whey powder
   (or noninstant milk
   powder)

some handfuls of
   granola
malt syrup to bind
¼ cup arrowroot,
   and/or whey or
   milk powder

Sprinkle wax paper with generous amount of milk powder or whey or arrowroot or all three.

Amalgamate the first four ingredients until you have a dough that is almost not sticky. Roll in the powder mix and shape into bars. Roll in more granola too, if desired.

Leave out in the open to harden. Then cover and refrigerate.

What's Good About It??

Soy powder is a very fine nonmeat protein source that gets even better when combined with nuts. And better *better* yet when combined with whey. Whey is a wide-spectrum nutrient. It is a high sodium food (known as the Youth Mineral, which you can take with a grain of salt, but anyway . . .), rich in milk sugar and friendly to the good bacteria that should be thriving in your intestinal tract if you're doing things right.

Another right thing to do is to use malt syrup, which is a superior source of phosphorus and a bit less sweet than comparable amounts of the other natural sweeteners.

Outstanding and it's mild.

SILLY PUTTY *(a seed taffy)*

1 cup raw sesame seeds	2 tbsp. sorghum syrup
½ cup oil (part sesame)	½ tsp. vanilla or almond extract

Put everything into blender, armed with a rubber spatula. Use this tool to keep seeds down. Let machine run a long time until mixture is glossy and putty-colored (and also hot). Turn out into bowl. With spatula, knead up on side of bowl, squeezing out oil. Finish kneading with your hands to squeeze out oil (save this for a future confectionary session). Either roll dough into log and slice into small pieces or pinch off knobs of dough and wrap individually in clear wrap.

What's Good About It??

Not the dextrosity that storebought saltwater (ha!) taffy turns out to be. Sesame seeds are a highly respectable source of B_{17} (also known as nitriloside) which aids in protecting against the degenerative diseases by bucking up the immunity system. (Since most cattle today are not fed their formerly lush grassy diet of yore, the resulting milk and cheese are almost invariably B_{17} deficient.) Another last lingering source of B_{17} is sorghum (remember it's a grass), so it is not always a surrogate for molasses, which has none.

One last aside about sesame: Did you know that just two tablespoons of sesame butter are equivalent in protein to a sixteen-ounce steak? It's a good seed indeed.

ODD BALLS *(a simplistic sweet)*

> 2 *cups of two kinds of raisins (hopefully, unsulphured)*
>
> 1 *tbsp. date syrup or blackstrap molasses (more if needed)*
>
> *dry-roasted nut flour (toast raw unsalted nuts in oven; then reduce them to flour by pulverizing in blender or seed mill)*
> *lavender leaves* *

Put the raisins through manual or electric food mill. Moisten with syrup and roll into little balls. Roll these balls in nut flour.

Serve on a bed of lavender leaves (if this is *too* simplistic a sweet for you).

* *See Source #1*

What's Good About It??

Seeded muscat grapes have a more pronounced flavor and are stickier than other kinds, so they'd be suitable here. Also, remember (the problem of pesticide residues aside), sun-dried fruit has a 30 percent increase in sugar content and it's in a form (fruit sugar) that can be assimilated without pre-digestion (like honey), so seek out the unsulphured varieties.

The lavender leaves, a nice fillip (a very old Latin tradition accounts for their use this way), are practical, too. When the company leaves, you can boil them up for a tea that's light and lively.

✓ **GOOD EARTH BARS** (*15 percent of your daily protein need in only two bars*)

½ cup real butter
½ cup peanut (or cashew) butter
1 cup real comb honey, beeswax and all
2 eggs
2 tsp. butter flavor extract
1 cup chopped peanuts, roasted or raw

2 cups whole wheat flour
¼ cup milk powder
1 tsp. salt
2 tsp. baking powder (aluminum-free)
½ cup milk
ground peanuts or any nut flour

Preheat oven to 350°. Cream together (in a capacious mixing bowl) nut butter and butter. When mixture is light, cream in honey. Beat in eggs one at a time, and then beat in extract. Stir together peanuts, flour, milk powder, salt and baking powder. Add this mixture alternately with the milk to creamed mixture.

Turn into two 9 x 9-inch oiled pans. Bake at 350°
for 25 miutes. Cool and cut into bars.

What's Good About It??

Something to own and mind along with your
own beeswax is butter, whose virtues are too often
belittled these cholesterol-conscious days. Did you
know that summer butter from cows fed fish-liver
oil may contain as much as 40,000 units of vitamin A
per pound (unit for unit, the vitamin A in butter
is more effective than the vitamin A in cod liver
oil)? Or, that the vitamin D found in a pound of
butter is equal to that found in ten quarts of milk?
Besides, butter is the most digestible and easily
tolerated of all fats. For the children, nothing could
be finer.

NO CREAM CREAMS

Organic Opera Creams

1 cup arrowroot and
  whey powders
1 cup drained
  yogurt *
1 cup light carob
  syrup
½ tsp. alginate

1 tsp. vanilla extract
¾ cup chopped nut-
  meats or meaty
  sprouts (sweet
  wheat sprouts
  would do)

Beat arrowroot and whey into yogurt. Heat syrup
with alginate and when well warmed, stir in the
creamed powders and beat. Add extract and nuts/

---

* Drained yogurt is fairly thick yogurt put into a triple
thickness of cheesecloth tied up like a sack and allowed to
drain at its leisure, suspended by some grocery string in your
kitchen. Save the whey and use the rest like sour cream.

sprouts. Spread in greased pan and chill thoroughly. Cut into "dainties" and eat between diets.

Organic Egg Cream

Put about one inch of hot light or dark carob syrup in a glass. Add about one inch of raw milk. Fill to the top with seltzered sassafras tea. (You'll need a seltzer bottle, which can sometimes be scared up in second-hand shops if you aren't equipped already.)

BREAKFAST IN A SINGLE GULP *(the Megavitamin Mug)*

2 *tbsp. ground sesame seeds*	1 *raw egg yolk*
1 *tbsp. sesame oil*	2 *tbsp. any natural sweetener*
1 *tbsp. raw wheat germ*	1 *tbsp. Sweet Nothing (see page 19)*
½ *cup yogurt*	1 *tbsp. food yeast*
4 *tbsp. skim milk powder*	1 *cup milk*

Blend the works and pour into a mighty mug for a super liquid breakfast.

What's Good About It??

This should suit you to a T because that's the vitamin it's rich in. Sesame seeds have, among their other virtues, the distinction of being one of the rare sources of vitamin T, which is largely responsible for keeping your spleen in splendid shape. Sesame seeds and sesame oil also contain a form of lecithin that is more readily usable by the body than soybean lecithin. Sesames are also about 21 percent iron. Isn't that uplifting?

See Recycling Note #1

THE COW'S MEOW *(not to be confused with the cat's pajamas)*

1 cup water, plain or fortified	1–2 tbsp. honey
1 tsp. catnip leaves	handful of alfalfa sprouts
1 cup buttermilk or cow's milk	

Heat water to boiling and pour over catnip. Infuse 10 minutes. Combine 1 cup of tea with remaining ingredients in blender. Process and drink warm or chilled. Good as a first-course creamed soup.

What's Good About It??

Catnip, like cow's milk, relaxes and promotes sound sleep. It is one of the oldest of herbal remedies, belonging to the mint and nettle family. And if you are blessed with more catnip leaves (it grows indoors or out quite easily in little pots), chop some for the salad bowl and don't forget a bouquet garni of it for pussy.

MU-MOO *(Chinese junk food? Definitely not)*

1 cup yogurt milk (half yogurt, half milk)	½ cup sunflower seed sprouts
1 cup Mu tea	2 tbsp. spicy honey (like basswood)

Combine tea with yogurt milk, sprouts and honey in blender. Process until smooth. Down the hatch.

What's Good About It??

Mu means infinity. Infinitely fascinating, it is a blend of sixteen rare herbs and seeds: ginseng, paonia root and coptis, to name an unusual few. And besides the protein from the moo juice, sunflower seeds provide you with more protein than any other vegetable seed. How now!

STICKUMS *(candy rich in C, E, F, calcium and lecithin)*

1 cup sesame seeds, unhulled	chopped dried currants
4 tbsp. honey or as needed	½ tsp. vanilla or fruit flavoring extract
¼ cup or as needed minced raisins or	walnut or pecan halves

Blend 1 cup of sesame seeds in the blender until they are a smooth mass. Knead on a floured surface (as you would a dough ball), working in a small amount of honey (the seeds have some natural sweetness, so don't overdo the honey), a handful of minced raisins or currants, a dash of pure vanilla or almond extract. When this is a compact ball, pinch off pieces, stickum with any nut halves you have, and chill briefly before serving.

SLIM PICKENS

¼ pound seedless raisins	2 ounces honey or sorghum
¼ pound dried apples	1 tbsp. lemon juice
2 tsp. organic fruit rind, grated	½ cup bran

Put fruits through a chopper or mill (using coarse blade) and mix with remaining ingredients. Mold mixture in pan. Chill. Shape into slim sucker shapes and spear with toothpicks.

See Recycling Note #4

YUM DROPS & POPS *(unfired unrefinery)*

¼ cup soy or dairy butter	alfalfa sprouts
¼ cup nut butter (peanut, cashew, almond, etc.)	wheat germ, raw
	½ ripe banana, mashed
6 tbsp. carob powder or dry malt powder	popcorn flour (freshly popped corn ground to a flour in blender)
6 tbsp. honey, date syrup or sorghum	food yeast
egg yolk	whey powder or milk powder
carrot, grated	cream cheese
flavoring extract	lecithin granules
raisins, minced	date chips or flakes
granola, ground	soy granules
sunflower seeds or peanuts, coarsely chopped	½ tsp. kelp powder
	unsweetened coconut
	popcorn flour

Combine butter, nut butter, carob and honey or other sweetener and mix until smooth. Add any of the remaining ingredients, except last two, in any amounts you like, adjusting balance of dry-wet ingredients with more fruit juice (if too dry) or more wheat germ (if too wet).

Shape into balls just barely sticky enough to pick up a coating. Roll in either or both of the last two ingredients.

For Yum Pops: Follow all above steps but lastly insert sucker stick in each ball, wrap in plastic wrap and chill.

PEPPERMINT STICKS

1 *pound basswood* *honey (peppermint* *flavor)*	*pinch cream of tartar* *or 1 tsp. vinegar*
5 *tbsp. water*	½ *tsp. peppermint es-* *sence or a few drops* *oil of peppermint* *

Slowly bring honey and water to boil and add cream of tartar or vinegar. Boil until a little of the mixture snaps when tested in cold water. Add peppermint and pour onto a greased plate. Leave until the edges take the mark of a finger. Fold the sides of the mixture into the center. Remove from plate and pull mixture till it lightens in color.

Cut into twelve to eighteen pieces and pull into sticks. Leave to set on a flat, greased surface.

What's Good About It??

Mass-produced peppermint sticks are funereal affairs. Their persuasive minty flavor and aroma will have come from some chemical whose origins it is better not to think too much about. This is better alchemy. In place of the unnatural stimulation of refined sugar, *mentha piperita* (peppermint to you) is a natural stimulant (pharmacologists have found it effective in stemming asthma attacks) and is very useful in all sorts of digestive disorders. So next time your tummy rumbles, reach for a sweet.

* *See Source #1*

A SPROUTED SWEET (*a cheapskate's own sweet, sprouted and steamed for good nutritional measure*)

¼ cup whole millet or millet grits
1 cup sprouted chick-peas
handful of raisins or currants (an extra)
1 egg white
1 slice of (hopefully homemade) whole wheat bread (if needed for bulk)
pinch of salt
pinch of nutmeg
2 ounces, or to taste, vanilla sugar or white "sugar"

Toast millet over moderate heat in skillet, stirring watchfully. Grind in blender. Grind chick-peas and raisins in food mill (or heavy-duty blender) and combine with millet. Add stiffly beaten egg white and sugar and seasoning. Roll into mite-sized balls and chill briefly. Pop into a steaming steamer and cook about 15 minutes. Yummy warm or cold.

What's Good About It??

Legume seeds (this includes chick-peas, of course) are 20 to 40 percent protein as a group (this is scandalously cheap protein, too) and when they are sprouted, their water content increases as much as 95 percent, an increment to consider because you probably didn't know that foods with a high water content are easier for the body to assimilate (and because the seeds have been sprouted they'll also yield as much as 33 percent more vitamin E than you'd get noshing the ungerminated garbanzo).

Note among millet's attributes that it is the most alkaline and easily digested of all the cereal grains (you'll find it very easy to digest the cost factor, too, since millet won't set you back much more than oatmeal). Steaming, of course, is a superior method of food preparation, and since no cookie sheets or oils or pans are called for, it sets you back nothing. See what they mean about the joy of cooking?

INSTANT CHOCOLATE-FREE CAKE MIX (jiffy-jar no-bowl method)

Put these in a Mason jar (or a large foil pouch):

¾ cup date sugar
¼ cup lecithin granules or flakes
½ cup raw sesame seeds, ground
½ cup carob powder

¼ cup wheat germ
1 tbsp. baking powder (aluminum-free)
½–1 tsp. any spice that suits your fancy

Keep this in refrigerator or freezer. When a dessert emergency arises: Put 3 eggs in blender, buzz, and add your mix packet, blending the first half and gradually adding what's left. If more oil is necessary, add ¼ cup. Bake in one cake pan or medium loaf pan at 325° (at this temperature the bottom won't scorch) for about 40 minutes, or until cake tests firm within.

INSTANT CHOCOLATE-FREE FROSTING (jiffy-jar bowl-free, too)

1 egg white
4 tbsp. any nonsolid natural sweetener

4 tbsp. arrowroot powder
1 tbsp. carob powder

Beat the white and mix in the other stuff. Put into a greased Mason jar (or refrigerator-freezer container) and store in freezer.

To thaw and use: Place jar in kettle of boiling water, turn kettle off and put lid on. When it has thawed, whip up, with the jar as your mixing bowl and using only one electric beater. For a thicker icing, add more arrowroot. For a chocolatey frosting, add more carob.

FIVE MINUTE FUDGE (*a "confection without objection" and best of all, it's uncooked*)

¼ cup soy butter
½ cup date syrup
½ cup carob powder
½ cup soy milk powder (or skim milk powder)

¼ cup food yeast or rice polish
1 tsp. vanilla extract
½ cup (more or less, it's up to you) granola

Cream butter and date syrup, spoon in other ingredients and blend well. Roll in more granola (for nuttier fudge) and press into a pan. Refrigerate. Cut into squares when properly chilled.

What's Good About It??

An important objection to any concentrated sweet is that it is acid-forming, a condition that taxes the body. Keeping the acid-alkaline balance just right at 20 percent to 80 percent is the basis of health. Innocent of all this is date syrup which is a nonacid-forming sweet. But curiously enough, taken in excess, dates will bring on constipation rather than diarrhea as you might suspect. With moderation then in mind, enjoy, enjoy this fudge which, thanks to the yeast (no, the children won't know it's there), the rice polish (ditto), the milk powder and the carob, is gloriously high in the full B-vitamin complex.

HOT ROCKS *(a sugarless and nutritionally superior peanut brittle)*

3 eggs	and/or low sodium,
1 cup honey	while you're at it)
1 cup sorghum	2 cups of mixed seeds
1 cup unrefined oil	and nuts (peanuts,
1 tsp. vanilla extract	sunflower seeds,
dash of almond extract	cashews and sesame,
1 tsp. baking powder	for instance—heavy
(aluminum-free	on the peanuts)

Put one cup of the mixture (comprising everything but the baking powder and nuts) into the blender. Save the rest for future candymaking bashes (it keeps well). Blend till smooth. Pour over the raw, unsalted, untoasted, partly chopped nuts and stir in baking powder. Pour into a large Pyrex casserole or onto a cookie pan (in either case, well buttered). Bake at 325–350° until candy is hard.

Break into Hot Rocks and eat hot, warm or cold.

What's Good About It??

The monkey-nut or ground nut (peanut to you) is not even a nut but a legume and one pound of them is equal nutritionally to two pounds of peas or three pounds of beefsteak, providing very good quality low-starch protein. Since surveys repeatedly show that 30 percent of schoolchildren tend to be deficient in iron, don't leave out the sorghum here. It ranks second only to liver as a source of that mighty mineral.

APPENDIX

APPENDIX

Charts

Sweeteners: Composition of Foods (100 Grams)

	Granulated sugar	Honey	Blackstrap molasses	Sorghum	Maple syrup	Maple sugar	Malt syrup	Date syrup
Food energy (calories)	385	304	213	160	252	294	367	274
Protein (gm)	0	0.3	0	98.98	—	—	6.0	2.2
Carbohydrates (gm)	99.5	82.3	55	77.1	65	100	89.2	72.9
Calcium (mg)	0	5	684	265.0	102	150	—	59
Phosphorus (mg)	0	6	84	16.0	8	10	—	63
Iron (mg)	0.1	0.5	16.1	1.76	1.2	1.6	4.0	3.0
Sodium (mg)	1	5	96	—	10	15	—	1
Potassium (mg)	3	51	2,927	—	176	260	—	648
Thiamin (mg)	0	trace	0.11	.10	—	—	.49	50
Riboflavin (mg)	0	0.04	0.19	.1	—	—	.31	.09
Niacin (mg)	0	0.3	2.0	—	—	—	9	.10
Vitamin C (mg)	0	1	0	—	—	—	—	2.2

Based on U.S. Department of Agriculture Handbook No. 8, *Composition of Foods.**

Before I say word one about sweeteners, make sure you've cast an eye at the preceding table. The federal government bears me out—white sugar is, to all intents and purposes, *nutrition-free*. Dashes indicate that there is no reliable data.

* Price $2.85 from the Superintendent of Documents, U.S. Government Printing Office, Washington, D.C. 20402. It's very worthwhile.

"The average consumption of honey is about one-and-one-half pounds per person per year. Most of us eat that much sugar in a week."

Vitamin content of territorial United States and foreign honeys (per 100 gm.).

Origin	Nectar Source	Thiamine	Riboflavin	Ascorbic Acid	Pyridoxine	Pantothenic Acid	Nicotinic Acid
U.S.A.		μg.	μg.	mg.	μg.	μg.	mg.
Washington	clover and alfalfa	6.8	67	1.5	227	96	.24
Washington	black locust	7.4	68	1.4	233	100	.47
Washington	fireweed	8.2	81	4.1	397	56	.13
Oregon	locust	4.3	35	5	260	103	.04
Oregon	alfalfa-sweet clover	4.3	36	1.3	430	175	.92
Oregon	fireweed	2.2	62	1.4	260	87	.84
Oregon	wild buck-wheat	4.3	56	2.8	250	180	.16
California (1941)	star thistle	8.6	137	6.5	410	90	.11
California (1941)	orange	8.6	35	2.5	210	150	.16
California	sage	3.0	36	5.4	320	56	.04
California	star thistle	3.0	58	1.3	420	58	.24
Texas	cotton	2.1	58	.6	350	103	.17
Texas	rattan	6.5	87	2.3	440	190	.23
Long Island	mixed	6.5	46	2.0	240	155	.26
Florida	tupelo	4.3	58	2.1	250	118	.44

Origin	Nectar Source	Thiamine	Riboflavin	Ascorbic Acid	Pyridoxine	Pantothenic Acid	Nicotinic Acid
New York (1936)	buckwheat	8.6	62	1.3	250	47	.13
Tennessee	poplar	6.5	–	1.2	240	–	.14
Tennessee	crimson clover	8.6	–	2.3	400	–	.56
Idaho	dandelion	6.4	87	2.5	267	192	.11
Montana	clover	3.3	77	3.2	416	141	.18
Montana	milkwort	9.1	–	2.9	250	–	.17
Minnesota	melon	7.1	36	2.6	400	156	.58
Minnesota	mixed	6.5	–	1.9	310	–	.11
Foreign		µg.	µg.	mg.	µg.	µg.	mg.
Greece	unknown	8.6	47	2.8	460	58	.16
France	lavender	6.4	145	2.5	410	112	.82
Czech'ia	linden	9.1	62	2.5	240	56	.04
Azores	unknown	2.2	81	2.6	250	150	.33
Haiti	logwood	3.0	65	1.5	280	50	.15
Cuba	campanilla	2.2	58	1.3	420	56	.67
Guatemala	coffee plant	7.1	62	2.5	250	60	.94

This table cannot be regarded as final, for several reasons. The vitamin content of a honey varies according to whether there has been a hot, dry season or a cold, wet one in the region where the blooms were grown from which the honeybees gather nectar. It is also affected by the chemical nature of the soil from which the flowers are grown. Moreover, there are times when the bees will consume nearly all of the pollen themselves and only a fractional amount will become blended with the honey they produce. Consequenty, one batch of honey from the same farm will have a higher vitamin C content at one time than at another.

"Clarifying honey
reduces the
vitamin content
up to 35–50%"

Composition of Honey

Amount per 100 gm.	Light Honey	Dark Honey
Calories	320	320
Copper, mg.	.030	.110
Iron, mg.	.24	1.28
Manganese, mg.	.33	.41
Thiamin, microgm.	5.5	5.5
Riboflavin, microgm.	61	61
Ascorbic acid, mg.	2.4	2.4
Nicotinic acid, mg.	.36	.36
Pantothenic acid, microgm.	105	105

The Nutritive Value of 1 Pound of Fruit

Fruit	Calories	Iron mg.	Potassium mg.	Vitamin A I.U.	Thiamin mg.	Riboflavin mg.	Niacin mg.	C mg.
Apple	234	1.3	459	380	.12	.08	.3	29
Apricot	217	2.1	1198	11510	.14	.16	2.6	42
Avocado	568	2.0	2055	990	.37	.67	5.4	48
Banana	262	2.2	1141	590	.14	.18	2.2	31
Blueberries	259	4.2	338	420	.13	.25	1.9	58
Cantaloupe	68	.9	569	7710	.10	.07	1.4	74
Cherries								
sour	242	1.7	797	4170	.21	.25	1.7	42
sweet	286	1.6	780	450	.20	.24	1.7	41
Figs	363	2.7	880	360	.29	.24	1.9	7
Mango	201	1.2	574	14590	.16	.16	3.2	106
Orange	162	1.3	662	660	.33	.13	1.3	166
Peach	150	2.0	797	5250	.17	.19	3.8	29
Pear	252	1.2	537	70	.09	.17	.6	18
Plum								
damson	272	2.1	1234	1240	.33	.13	2.2	—
prune	320	2.1	725	1280	.14	.14	2.3	17
Strawberries	161	4.4	714	260	.12	.29	2.6	257
Watermelon	54	1.0	209	1230	.06	.06	.3	15

What One Cup of Pure Orange Juice Will Give You

Nutrient	Amount	What It Does for You	Needed in Human Nutrition
Water	88%	Maintains body temperature, enters into bloodstream, all hormones and body systems.	YES
Calories	110	Provides healthful energy and natural vitality to boost vigor and strength.	YES
Protein	2 grams	Essential component of all living cells. Builds, maintains and repairs all body tissues. Supplies energy. Helps form antibodies to fight infection. Forms important part of enzymes, hormones, body fluids.	YES
Carbohydrates	26 grams	Supplies energy. Helps the body use fats more effectively. Needed for body warmth. Aids digestive tract by adding bulk.	YES
Calcium	27 mgs.	Builds bones and teeth. Helps blood to clot. Helps functioning of muscles, nerves and heart.	YES
Iron	.5 units	Combines with protein to make hemoglobin, the red substance of blood that carries oxygen to all body cells. Helps cells use oxygen and develop energy.	YES

continued . . .

Vitamin A	500 units	Helps keep skin smooth and soft. Aids eyesight. Protects against night blindness. Helps keep mucous membranes (lining) of mouth, nose, throat and digestive tract healthy and resistant to infection.	YES
Vitamin B1 (Thiamine)	.22 mgs.	Needed for proper function of heart and nervous system. Helps obtain energy from food.	YES
Vitamin B2 (Riboflavin)	.07 mgs.	Needed for healthy skin. Helps prevent sensitivity of eyes to light. Needed to build and maintain healthy body tissues.	YES
Niacin	1.0 mgs.	Helps convert food to energy. Aids nervous system and helps prevent appetite loss. Works with enzymes.	YES
Vitamin C	124 mgs.	Helps keep bone, teeth, blood vessels healthy. Helps build strong bone structure. Helps distribute calcium for fine tooth formation. Builds resistance to cold and respiratory allergies.	YES
Potassium	460 mgs.	Helps maintain cell fluid balance. Permits normal nerve impulse conduction. Helps muscles contract. Regulates acid-alkaline balance.	YES
Magnesium	22 mgs.	Relaxes nerves, promotes new cells, activates enzymes. Helps form body proteins. Regulates temperature.	YES
Phosphorus	43 mgs.	Works with calcium to form and maintain bones, teeth. Found in nucleus of each cell. Aids in metabolism of carbohydrates.	YES

"Fruit Sugars are found in all fruits and are really the only ones that the body can digest and assimilate. While they are not quite so sweet, they are quickly and readily digested and pass right into the circulation. In case one does not eat a sufficient amount of Fruit Sugars, Nature can manufacture her own grape sugar from the starches eaten."

Pan American Diet Book
G. W. REMNSBURG

What One Cup of "Instant Breakfast Drink" Will Give You
(IMITATION ORANGE FLAVOR)

Ingredient	Functions	Needed in Human Nutrition
Sugar	Adds calories. Offers erratic bursts of energy.	NO
Citric Acid	Obtained from chemicalized fermentation processes. Gives a high acid flavor. May affect teeth and bone enamel.	NO
Natural Flavor	Chemically prepared flavor from real or artificial sources to duplicate the natural flavor of the product represented.	NO
Gum Arabic (Vegetable Gum)	A plant gum that acts like a mucilage. May cause allergic reaction or intestinal irregularities.	NO
Monosodium Phosphate	An emulsifier and sequestrant (binds and inactivates minerals). Also known as sodium biphosphate. High sodium content. Chemical source.	NO
Potassium Citrate	A sodium salt of citric acid. It acts as a sequestrant, emulsifier, buffer or acidifier. Also known as sodium citrate. High sodium content. Chemical source.	NO
Calcium Phosphate	Prevents caking. Refined and purified chemical. A strong caustic. May cause allergic reaction or intestinal distress.	NO

Vitamin C	Usually from a synthetic source. May be a coal tar derivative.	YES
Cellulose Gum	Usually from a vegetable source. A natural plant gum. May cause allergic or intestinal reaction.	NO
Hydrogenated Coconut Oil	High saturated fat that predisposes to cholesterol-atherosclerosis buildup in body's arteries. Provides "thickness" and "body" to the beverage.	NO
Ferrous Sulfate	A chemically reduced iron powder (iron oxide reduced by the addition of hydrogen). If strong enough, may be poisonous to youngster; may also cause liver damage.	NO
Artificial Flavor	Gives an orange flavor. Usually from a chemical source.	NO
Artificial Color	Gives the beverage the look of orange juice. Makes it look like the real thing.	NO
Vitamin A	Usually from a synthetic source. May be a coal tar derivative. Gives consumer an illusion of nutritive value.	YES
BHA Preservative	Known fully as butylated hydroxyanisole. A coal tar product. Used as an antioxidant in the flavor. May have cancer forming properties.	NO

"When taken into the body Granulated Sugar breaks down the cells in order to furnish the blood with the necessary alkaline elements to neutralize the carbonic acid which is formed in the oxidation of the carbon of which Sugar is composed. . . ."

Pan American Diet Book
G. W. REMNSBURG

Recycling Notes

1. One cup will replace the milk in Honey Buns (page 84) or part of the cream in Herbal Ice Cream (page 65). Or, what's to stop you from sloshing the remains on tomorrow's cold cereal?

2. (Sugarless Ice Cream Cones) Crush or crumble and toss into your granola cannister. Or use ¼ cup coarsely crushed cone crumbs to replace nuts in any cookie recipe.

3. Use wherever a small amount of fruity sweetening is needed. Try it as the sweet inner lining for Brown-and-Serve Sweet Rolls (page 67).

4. Soften leftover candy to room temperature, or heat at 200° for 10 minutes and use ¼ to ½ cup to replace that amount of dried fruit in Hasty Pudding (page 70).

5. (Baby's Formula) To make sweet, nourishing noodles, use ¼ cup of this and add enough whole wheat flour for a moderately stiff dough. Roll out to ⅛-inch thickness, dry, cut into noodles, dry again on wax paper. Simmer 10 minutes in small amount of water or milk (save this for thickening sauces).

6. Use ½ cup leftover porridge to replace ½ cup flour in Good Earth Bars (page 160) and reduce milk to ¼ cup.

7. Whip 1 cup water with 1 tbsp. gelatin (warm water first) in blender until very frothy. Pour over leftover frosting and fold in 1 stiffly beaten egg white. Chill and have for dessert (now that the cookies or cake that frosting went on is gone, you'll need *something*).

8. Stretch a skimpy cookie dough (the drop not roll kind) by beating in the batter left from breakfast.

9. Make sassy "Jell-O." Instead of fruit juice and gelatin, substitute leftover rootbeer, and jell as usual.

10. Put into any pancake batter and adjust liquid or substitute for part of the yogurt cream in Waffle Cookies (page 95).

11. Yogurt's qualities begin to diminish after a week but if you still have some on day eight, put it in the blender with an equal amount of dried fruits. Whip and chill for a Quick Sherbet.

12. Put ½ cup into almost any drop cookie recipe, or replace the nuts ordered in any muffin formula.

13. (Basic Baby's Bread) If you made bread, not buns, slice the loaf that's left (and threatening to go stale) and slice each slice into thirds. Place these on a rack or cookie sheet and toast leisurely (an hour or more) in a low (300°, maybe even 275°) oven till very dry. Should keep nicely in a covered cannister. Good teething things.

14. (Frosty Flakes) Leftover ready-to-eat cereal like this can replace the nuts in almost any recipe (if you're short in the cash or cashew department).

15. (Seven Upper) These dregs are dandy poured cold over your morning granola, rather than milk. Another rather: Heat the dregs and have them poured over some blender-ground granola for a fast hot cereal.

16. (Sugarfree Strufoli) The last forgotten few make a fine streusellike topping for soft desserts like

Hasty Pudding (page 70) or Slush Piles (page 62). Crumble and sprinkle.

17. (Herbal Ice Cream) Let what's left self-liquify, and use in place of the milk or sweet liquid specified in any pudding or cake recipe.

18. (Slush Piles) Like to make some cheap-jack applejack? Put the apple peelings (assuming they are unsprayed) into a saucepan with a small amount of water and a piece of cinnamon stick. Bring to a boil, simmer briefly, strain.

19. (Wonder Whip) What whip went wanting can be put in the blender with a bit of water, liquified, and then used in place of the fortified water so often specified in this book (and you may also want to cut back on the sweetness in that recipe when you do).

20. (Arf-and-Arf) Luxurious chemical-free way to soften up a tough steak. Bathe your beef in this leftover yogurt and keep in refrigerator a full day (turning occasionally).

21. (Grinder Jam) A second life for such sweet stuff: spread over dough for Brown-and-Serve Sweet Rolls (page 67), omitting the chopped mixed fruits. Proceed as directed.

22. (Sugar-free Protein Drink) Cook your rice (for the children if not yourself) in an equivalent amount of this rather than water. Swell snack, breakfast or side dish.

23. (Chocolate Spaghetti) Would you believe these leftovers are one step away from new waffles? Blend the remains with 1 or 2 large tablespoons of plain yogurt and add to your standard waffle recipe (adding an extra whipped white if your recycled pasta makes more than ⅔ cup).

24. (Blackstrap Branola) For Blackstrap Brittle, heat 2 cups of date sugar in heavy skillet, stirring until sugar becomes syrupy. Add cereal. Pour onto cold oiled platter. Break into pieces when cold.

25. Save the used tea leaves. When dried they can be used to stuff homemade cloth toys at Christmastime. Leftover marinade can replace part of the stock in your next spicy beef stew.

Sources

Always check first with your local natural food shops or gourmet grocery stores for supplies. When all else fails, try the below.

	SOURCES	FOR . . .
#1	Aphrodisia 28 Carmine St. New York, N.Y. 10014	herbs and spices (send 25 cents for cata- log)
	Nature's Herb Co. 281 Ellis St. San Francisco, Cal. 94102	
#2	Asian Express P.O. Box 375 Pelham, N.Y. 10803	bean sprouts, tofu, sea- weed, five-spice pow- der, fresh ginger, etc. (write for free listings)
#3	Walnut Acres Penns Creek, Pa. 17862	grains, flour, honeys, and much more (write for free catalogs)
	Arrowhead Mills, Inc. Box 866 Hereford, Tex. 79045	

	SOURCES	FOR . . .
#4	W. Atlee Burpee Riverside, Cal. 92502	seeds for sprouting (specify untreated) (free catalogs)
	Joseph Harris Co. Rochester, N.Y.	
#5	Waconia Sorghum Co. Cedar Rapids, Iowa	sorghum syrup (write for ordering information)
#6	Infinity Company 171 Duane St. New York, N.Y. 10013	date syrup in cans, jars and drums (write for prices)
#7	Eleanor Levitt 270 W. Merrick Rd. Valley Stream, N.Y.	dripless honey pourer (glass dispenser)
#8	Hires, Int'l. Evanston, Ill. 60202	root beer extract (or try your local winemaker's supplies shop)
#9	Rising Sun Publications 25 Exeter St. Boston, Mass. 02116	"Sprouting for Economy" pamphlet
#10	Wayside Industries Marlborough, Mass. 01752	Irish moss (8-ounce package, less than one dollar)
#11	John Wagner & Sons Ivyland, Pa. 18974	extensive line of pure fruit extracts (free catalog)

Index